Sport, Fun and Enjoyment

Sport, Fun and Enjoyment explores the pleasurable aspects of sport within the context of everyday recreational and competitive physical activities. While much recent work has focused on the relationships between physical activity, health and wellbeing, much less attention has been paid to pleasure and fun, key aspects of our engagement with sport but not so easy to measure in terms of specific outcomes. By offering a critical exploration of what can be constituted as 'fun' in a sporting context, this book reveals the complex ways in which individuals approach sport and engage with it throughout the lifecourse.

The book considers the importance of pleasure and fun as a factor in our initial, formative experiences of sport activity, and as a factor in participation and continued participation. It explores the nature of fun as an embodied experience which incorporates a multitude of social, psychological and physiological components, and as a subjective experience which cannot be fully explained through simplistic binary formulations of pleasure and pain. Drawing on wide research literature and original empirical research with children and adults, the book outlines a new theoretical framework for thinking about pleasure and fun in sport, highlighting the contrasting ways in which sport and physical activity are experienced and the interplay between individual and social contexts.

Sport, Fun and Enjoyment is important reading for anybody with an interest in physical education, youth sport, the sociology of sport, physical activity and health, sport development or sport policy.

Ian Wellard is a Reader in the Sociology of Sport and Physical Education. His main research interests relate to body practices, masculinities, and sport. Recent books include *Sport, Masculinities and the Body* and *Rethinking Gender and Youth Sport*, both for Routledge.

Routledge Studies in Physical Education and Youth Sport
Series Editor: David Kirk
University of Bedfordshire, UK

The *Routledge Studies in Physical Education and Youth Sport* series is a forum for the discussion of the latest and most important ideas and issues in physical education, sport, and active leisure for young people across school, club and recreational settings. The series presents the work of the best well-established and emerging scholars from around the world, offering a truly international perspective on policy and practice. It aims to enhance our understanding of key challenges, to inform academic debate, and to have a high impact on both policy and practice, and is thus an essential resource for all serious students of physical education and youth sport.

Also available in this series

Physical Literacy
Throughout the lifecourse
Edited by Margaret Whitehead

Physical Education Futures
David Kirk

Young People, Physical Activity and the Everyday
Living physical activity
Edited by Jan Wright and Doune Macdonald

Muslim Women and Sport
Edited by Tansin Benn, Gertrud Pfister and Haifaa Jawad

Inclusion and Exclusion Through Youth Sport
Edited by Symeon Dagkas and Kathleen Armour

Sport Education
International perspectives
Edited by Peter Hastie

Cooperative Learning in Physical Education
An international perspective
Edited by Ben Dyson and Ashley Casey

Equity and Difference in Physical Education, Youth Sport and Health
A narrative approach
Edited by Fiona Dowling, Hayley Fitzgerald and Anne Flintoff

Game Sense
Pedagogy for performance, participation and enjoyment
Richard Light

Ethics in Youth Sport
Policy and pedagogical applications
Stephen Harvey and Richard Light

Assessment in Physical Education
A sociocultural perspective
Peter Hay and Dawn Penney

Complexity Thinking in Physical Education
Reframing curriculum, pedagogy and research
Edited by Alan Ovens, Tim Hopper and Joy Butler

Pedagogies, Physical Culture, and Visual Methods
Edited by Laura Azzarito and David Kirk

Contemporary Developments in Games Teaching
Edited by Richard Light, John Quay, Stephen Harvey and Amanda Mooney

Sport, Fun and Enjoyment
An embodied approach
Ian Wellard

Sport, Fun and Enjoyment

An embodied approach

Ian Wellard

LONDON AND NEW YORK

First published 2014
by Routledge
2 Park Square, Milton Park, Abingdon, Oxon OX14 4RN

and by Routledge
711 Third Avenue, New York, NY 10017

Routledge is an imprint of the Taylor & Francis Group, an informa
business

British Library Cataloguing in Publication Data
A catalogue record for this book is available from the British Library

Library of Congress Cataloging-in-Publication Data
Wellard, Ian.
Sport, fun and enjoyment : an embodied approach / by Ian Wellard.
pages cm. -- (Routledge studies in physical education and youth sport)
1. Sports--Sociological aspects. 2. Sports--Psychological aspects. I. Title.
GV706.5.W456 2013
306.4'83--dc23
2013016567

ISBN: 978-0-415-64097-8 (hbk)
ISBN: 978-0-203-08234-8 (ebk)

Typeset in Times New Roman
by Fakenham Prepress Solutions, Fakenham, Norfolk NR21 8NN

Contents

List of figures and tables

Figures

Table

Acknowledgements

I would like to thank Routledge for their continued support.

Although there are many who have helped shape my thinking throughout the writing process, I would like to mention Steve, Adesola, Gemma, James and Marion in particular. I would also like to acknowledge all the children and adults who kindly took part in conversations and interviews during the various research projects included in this book.

Lastly, but most importantly, I would like to thank John and Toby for always being there and remember Dad, who helped me enjoy sport much more than I had realised.

1 Introduction

Sport and embodied pleasures

When I was about eight years old, my dad would take my brother and me to the local swimming pool every Saturday morning. It was a regular event which marked the start of the weekend, but was something I looked forward to all week. It was time to be with my dad, as he was always busy during the weekdays, and a time for swimming which was fun time. Swimming at school was ok, but it wasn't the same as going to the public pool on a Saturday morning. This was special. The pool opened its doors at 8.30 and we would always make sure we were down there by 8.15 so that we could be first in the queue. Not that there was usually anyone else there, but just in case. I would always hurry everyone along as I wanted to be there first. My reason was so that I could enjoy one of the highlights of the visit – being the first one in the pool. My brother would sometimes put up a challenge and try to race me, but I had developed an art of being able to get changed in minutes. Clothes were off and thrown in the basket before my dad had finished paying for our tickets. It was an old Victorian swimming pool where the changing rooms were downstairs, arranged in rows of cubicles with a central area where you would leave your basket of clothing with the attendant who would exchange it for a rubber bracelet with a number on. I would always put this around my ankle as I didn't like it moving around my skinny wrist. I could never remember the face of the attendant, only a glimpse of a hand from which I snatched the wristband. I was too concerned to get up the steps to the pool as quickly as possible and be the one to have the first go at breaking the seal of the water. There was something magical about the water when it was completely still. It was fresh, calm and unbearably enticing. By getting there first, not only did it feel like the pool was mine – but I had the choice of how I would break the seal. I could dive, in an attempt to enter with as little disturbance as possible and then be able to swim underneath the still surface. Or, in most cases, I could do a massive bomb and try to make as much disruption to the stillness as possible. Regardless of how I chose to enter the water, it was a time when the pool belonged to me. Having my own personal water world

would only last for a minute or so until my brother or some other intruder
jumped in. But it was a moment I savoured and knew I could repeat next
Saturday.

(A personal reflection upon a childhood experience)

My childhood memories of sport, the ones that I remember most vividly and
with most affection, are those that incorporated movement, imagination, play,
adventure and excitement. They occurred outside school, with my dad and
brothers or with my friends. As an older teenager, they were at sports clubs.
School sport was less enjoyable and something that I realised had to be tolerated,
as the PE teachers were only interested in the boys who were good at football. I
can remember that I understood sporting activity in terms of a clear distinction
between the activities I took part in outside school that were fun and the PE
lessons that were distinctly not. Consequently, the majority of the memories that I
have of childhood sport and physical activity are located outside the school gates,
and I find it hard to remember anything distinctive about school PE, apart from
my indifference to the PE teachers because of their preoccupation with football.
There was also an irony that I had not considered at the time. My dad had been a
keen football player in his youth and had, at one stage, managed a local football
team. However, unlike the PE teachers, he was a keen all-round sportsman and
encouraged me to take part in any sport so long as I enjoyed it.

These brief personal accounts are included as they have helped me establish
questions in relation to what it is that individuals 'get out of' taking part in
recreational sport and physical activity. In seeking to understand what it was that
made me continue to take part as an adult, I am constantly returning to questions
about what is it that constitutes a pleasurable experience and how this experience
resonates enough to make an individual want to do it again. Consequently, the
main focus for this book is to explore the pleasurable aspects of sport within the
context of everyday recreational and competitive physical activities.

Although much recent focus in the public domain on the 'health' and 'wellbeing'
of individuals has brought thinking about abstract concepts such as pleasure and
happiness to the fore, within the context of sport the benefits for taking part are
more likely considered in terms of outcomes related to better health and positive
citizenship. Pleasure or 'fun' are not so easy to measure in terms of specific
outcomes and are only usually considered as an additional bonus. Research
constantly highlights 'fun' as a major factor in the positive experience of both
children and adults (MacPhail *et al.* 2003, Wright 2004, Dismore and Bailey
2011) although the specific manifestation of fun is rarely elaborated upon. Indeed,
it is more often than not dismissed as *just* fun (McNamee 2005, Bloodworth *et*
al. 2012). However, critical exploration of what can be constituted as fun reveals
the complex ways in which individuals approach sport and physical activity.
Indeed, a general understanding of fun, if considered within a wellbeing frame, is
less clear when some aspects of sport, such as extreme sports and combat sports,
may be considered fun by the participants and potentially contribute to their
own individual wellbeing, while for others the activities might be considered

hazardous to health. Similarly, at professional level, in the quest for achievement and success, the use of extreme regimes of training, performance-enhancing drugs (sanctioned or illegal) and modified diets are not necessarily healthy and may not be regarded by participants as intrinsically positive or pleasurable (Heikkala 1993, Pronger 2002). For instance, the tennis player Andre Agassi's revelations in his autobiography about 'hating' tennis are a case in point:

> *I play tennis for a living, even though I hate tennis, hate it with a dark and secret passion, and always have.*
>
> (Agassi 2009: 3)

The subjective experience of 'hating' something may be more tolerable if the outcome is considered worthwhile. Agassi's hate can be seen to be alleviated by the (presumably enjoyable) economic rewards and possibly understood in the knowledge that his relationship to sport is very much framed in a traditional work-recreation binary where playing tennis is considered work. Constant reference to professional sports players and elite athletes can, therefore, be misleading when attempting to explore the broader dimensions of fun and enjoyment. Although professional sports players are invariably positioned as the pinnacle of sporting achievement, on examination the practices they adhere to are not necessarily relevant to the majority of the population for whom sporting activities are undertaken voluntarily and with an expectation of enjoyment, albeit in multifarious ways. Central to a sport player's status as 'professional' is that their participation is related to it being their main source of income and their focus is based upon the outcome of 'winning'. This provides the framework for their training and continued participation. A more useful question to be posed to Agassi and professional sports players in general might relate to what they find enjoyable in sports other than their own. For instance, in a series of articles about Olympic athletes' 'passions', the British long jumper Chris Tomlinson described his love of golf:

> *I absolutely love golf. I would rather play golf than do athletics... What appeals to me about golf – apart from being outside – is that you can switch off the phone and for hours focus only on your next shot.*
>
> (Interview with Chris Tomlinson, *The Times*, 3 March 2012)

The orientation to the sporting activity is obviously crucial. For Tomlinson, like many other recreational sports participants, the activity is a means to 'escape', which ultimately shapes the way in which the sport is approached.

More recent discourses of obesity, or as David Kirk (2006) describes it, the 'obesity crisis', have also shifted greater attention on the role of recreational sport and exercise as part of a weight-loss programme. However, whereas an obese person may enter into a punishing exercise programme with the motivation (or hope) of losing weight, this form of reasoning may be less persuasive for a child or an adult for whom health is not necessarily considered problematic. Rather, it would be more likely that enjoyment (in its multiple immeasurable, subjective forms) is a central motivation. Consequently, whereas sport *and* achievement and wellbeing *and* heath are often used in tandem, they are not necessarily synonymous with each other. However, the central argument presented in this book is that a focus upon fun, enjoyment and pleasure in sport provides opportunities to reveal the contrasting and complex relationships that individuals develop toward sport and physical activity, and, ultimately, any subsequent 'assessments' of wellbeing.

Fun (incorporating pleasure and enjoyment) is, therefore, considered important in relation to being:

1   a significant factor in participation and continued participation;
2   a major factor in initial experiences of sporting activity;
3   a subjective experience which cannot be fully explained in terms of acts which are intrinsically hedonistic or defined through simplistic binary formulations of pleasure and pain;
4   an embodied experience which incorporates a multitude of social, psychological and physiological components.

Embodied experience, for an individual taking part in a sporting activity, has tended to be interpreted in terms of the physiological effects of exertion, with the release of endorphins being the main channel for what could tenuously be described as pleasure. However, more recent theorising of the experience of the sportsperson has offered ways in which the concept of physical pleasure should be incorporated in any analysis of the sporting body. For instance, recent work in sport psychology has drawn upon the ideas of Csikszentmihalyi (1990) in order to explore the idea of 'flow' which could be considered not only a psychological state of being but also a physiological one. This sense of physical and mental 'well-being' has also found favour in recent government thinking and has generated discussion about the contribution of sport to individual wellbeing (Bailey *et al.* 2007). However, much of this debate has tended to focus on the elite athlete and ignore subjective interpretations of wellbeing and the influence of philosophical and sociological thinking on how it is in fact determined (Vernon 2008). Consequently, and even more significantly when exploring the meaning of sporting activity in the life of a social (amateur) sports participant, although abstract concepts such as happiness and pleasure are necessary equations within any consideration of wellbeing, they are mostly ignored.

The intention, therefore, is to propose a theoretical frame for thinking about fun and enjoyment within the context of sport. The starting point is very much grounded in a sociological framework which sees pleasure and fun as being socially constructed. However, it is recent work emerging from phenomenological approaches to 'embodied' thinking (Allen-Collinson 2009, Smith *et al.* 2007) as well as physiology (Booth 2009) and psychological explorations of affect and happiness (Ahmed 2010) and shame (Probyn 2005) that clearly influences the ways in which these concepts can be further contemplated.

In an attempt to pull these ideas together, Raewyn Connell's (2005) description of 'body-reflexive practices' is adopted as a mechanism for starting to develop a theoretical frame that incorporates an embodied approach to the sporting body and includes social, psychological and physiological recognition of individual experience. Connell's arguments are important as they form the basis of an understanding of the significance of the social and physical body and bodily practices. Body-reflexive practices are, she argues, formed through a circuit of bodily experiences which link to bodily interaction and bodily experience via socially constructed bodily understandings which lead to new bodily interactions. As a result, Connell continues, social theory needs to account for the corporeality of the body. 'Through body-reflexive practices, bodies are addressed by social process and drawn into history, without ceasing to be bodies... they do not turn into symbols, signs or positions in discourse' (Connell 2005: 64). Connell's concept of body-reflexive practices helps us understand how social and cultural factors interact with individual experiences of the body. This in turn creates a need to recognise not only the social forms and practices which underpin the individual's ability to take part in sport, or any other physical activity, but also the unique experiences or physical thrill of body-based expression.

Reflexivity

I draw upon the concept of reflexivity heavily, not only in terms of methodo-logical process, but importantly as a way of conceptualising the social through a constant reflection upon the social and psychological influences which shape the way that I react to the world and attempt to understand it. I have attempted to weave in the personal as it has (like anyone else) shaped my relationship to sport; although I am mindful that it is not the only influence. Recent popularity of the personal voice, through biographical approaches (for example, Stanley 1993, Sparkes 2002), has enabled more qualitative examination of the subjective personal experience. However, in terms of generating understanding about broader society, I am less interested in myself as a focus, unless it is as part of a reflexive approach to the development of the research questions or the methodo-logical decision making. As Plummer states, 'the starting point is always the social' (Plummer 2010: 18) and, as a consequence, social research is about *others* and finding out about how other people have formed and constructed knowledge and ways to interact with others. This simplistic theoretical and methodological starting point was a reason that I was attracted to sociology in the first place. I had ideas that I had developed about myself and my place within society and these had generated many questions. However, I felt that I needed to explore the lives of other people (individuals and groups) in order to reassess those questions. At the same time, the intention underlying my research was to reassure myself that I was not living in a vacuum of my own thoughts, as I had presumed that it was more likely that my thinking was not unique. So, in order to answer questions, I needed to 'observe' the world and focus upon 'others'. As such, I have only considered myself important in terms of my reflexive contribution to the research process, both in terms of my theoretical and methodological position (Bourdieu and Wacquant 1992). Consequently, my theoretical starting point is embedded in attempts to observe or engage with an empirical reality where acknowledging the subjective in terms of the reflexive stance of the researcher within the research process is crucial. *However*, making the researcher the sole focus of the research significantly distorts the possibilities for making attempts at observing empirical reality. My own methodological approach, influenced by my sociological training, (as well as a psychological unease about wanting to be the centre of attention) has shaped the way that I 'do' research.

Ethnography has been an important aspect of my research, in the sense that it is in the present as part of an exploratory form of investigation into the social. Auto-ethnography is considered in this way as an extension of the exploration which takes into account the emotional experiences encountered during the research process. Reflection is incorporated as part of the analysis of the experiences alongside the reflexive awareness of one's personal agenda. Consequently, the past is important, as reflective accounts, in the historical sense, are key elements of the material gathered about the individuals or groups which form the focus for the investigation. I am thinking here in particular of life-history interviews, such as those conducted by Connell (2005) and Plummer (1983), or documented evidence, such as diaries and artworks. All of which can be analysed as part of an ethnographic exploration of the social and written up as a means of telling a 'convincing story' (Silverman 1989).

However, as much as I acknowledge my sociological lens, this need not be to the detriment of my own subjectivity. Throughout this book, I have drawn upon personal reflections which have helped me develop questions about 'how' and 'why' other people may approach sport and experience it. In particular, these reflections and those of the people I have researched in the past are very much influenced by the emotional. Indeed, as Ian Burkitt rightly suggests, emotion

> is not just something that we reflect upon in a disengaged way, it is central to the way people in social relations relate to one another: it is woven into the fabric of the interactions we are engaged in and it is therefore also central to the way we relate to ourselves as well as to others.
>
> (Burkitt 2012: 459)

Burkitt highlights the emotional dimensions of reflexivity and how it is more than just a methodological stance that allows the researcher to 'stand back' from their own world and effectively monitor and manage emotions. Much of this influence in methodological approach can be witnessed in recent thinking related to emotional intelligence, where the intention is to 'manage' or contain emotions which may negatively affect work performance. According to Burkitt, theories of reflexivity have been developed through a Cartesian stance where, 'a knowledgeable agent stands at an emotional distance from the social world and makes reflexive choices on the basis of their knowledge' (2012: 461). Emotions or feelings are separate from a knowledge base which informs decisions. For Burkitt, this understanding of reflexivity is not a relation, but disembodied. Reflexivity is understood and based in knowledge where 'it is not a given but is based on self-reflection which emerges from the reflective dialogues that humans hold with themselves' (2012: 462).

Importantly, what Burkitt tells us is that emotions are not necessarily a subjective limitation of the individual, that need to be kept in check via a disengaged management system, but rather, they are shaped and formed *within* the knowledge structures that an individual is exposed to. Burkitt's ideas resonate with Sartre's discussion of 'being', especially in relation to the notion of being-for-others. As Burkitt describes,

> We are emotionally engaged with others in our social interactions and these emotional engagements regularly motivate our reflexivity through the reflexive dialogue and privately staged with the image and voice of others.
>
> (Burkitt 2012: 469)

Thus the reflections of my trip to the swimming pool as a child highlight a range of factors: the sensual feelings of the body in movement, the thrill of the body confronting natural elements and the excitement of the physical body with other bodies in the context of a (constructed) social event such as a visit to a public swimming pool. However, what is important is that my experiences of childhood swimming were a combination of anticipation, experience and reflection, a process that shaped and contributed to a lifelong disposition toward sport and physical activity. Consequently, I am suggesting that fun and enjoyment in sport is more than just an intrinsic, subjective, highly individual experience. These ideas have been developed during previous research exploring the body and sport (Wellard 2006b, 2007, 2009) where themes relating to bodily pleasure, fun and enjoyment as elements in sporting participation constantly appeared in the narratives of the interviewees. Although in these cases, the specific theme of fun and enjoyment was not the original research aim, it emerged as a significant factor in the respondents' justification for continuing to participate in sport.

In addition to my previous research relating to embodied aspects of gender, involvement in several large-scale, funded projects exploring sporting participation in children and young people has added support to my claim that young people need to have a range of experiences of sport in order to make distinctions about what can be considered pleasurable for them. Many of the ideas put forward in this book have been influenced by my observations and conversations during research in schools and sport-related projects in the last ten years[1]. Much of this research has involved visiting schools and community-based schemes throughout England, Scotland and Wales. Indeed, during this time, I have visited over 50 schools and over 20 different community sport clubs, several on more than one occasion. My experiences while visiting these schools and clubs, like my research with a range of men in sports clubs (Wellard 2009), have made me continually reconsider my theoretical position, particularly in relation to thinking about what is in fact beneficial for children and adults in terms of sport provision. As I have previously stated (Wellard 2006a, 2009), there is often a disparity between the claims of theory and the lived realities of those at 'ground level'. Although the tensions between theory and practice (and praxis) are not new, they are still a cause of conflict and can often be seen to create unnecessary divisions as those with vested interests feel the need to 'take sides'.

Throughout my experiences conducting research within schools, it has been constantly apparent that young people do not always have the same opportunities and levels of provision. Research conducted by the Centre for Sport, Physical Education and Activity Research (SPEAR) has highlighted that participation in sport remains dependent upon a range of arbitrary and competing factors. For example, between 2010 and 2012, SPEAR was involved in evaluations of two high-profile national interventions aimed at increasing sports participation among young people (The Bank of Scotland and Lloyds TSB National School Sport Week and the Change 4 Life School Sports Clubs programme). The overall findings from the research suggest that these large-scale initiatives were generally considered positive experiences and, importantly, the children taking part enjoyed having the opportunity to try new or unusual sports, regardless of whether they said they liked sport to begin with. The research also revealed, however, disparities between what adults and children wanted from such events and contrasting interpretations of what a school sports week or a specific sport club could offer and how it could be integrated into the schools. In the case of the National School Sport Week, the research also revealed that primary schools appeared more willing and flexible to incorporate a whole-school approach, whereas secondary schools tended to locate the event within a Physical Education department and focus more upon the competitive aspects found within tradi-tional sports. Consequently, the contrasting ways in which these initiatives were embraced within schools highlighted that not all schools are always sufficiently willing and/or able to deliver quality sports provision in uniform ways and also provide novel and creative opportunities for all children.

However, these events, like school sport in general are not just about providing the opportunity to 'have a go' in order to comply with curriculum directives. They are about providing opportunities for young people to experience activities and make assessments about when, where and how an activity is enjoyable. The important point here is about recognising the influence of fun and enjoyment for young people in their initial experiences of sport and subsequent formation of a sporting identity. Although, as adults, we may be aware of the benefits of partici-pating in sport and physical activities, those benefits are not necessarily obvious for children. In particular, there is the risk of complacency among PE teachers, as it is easy to forget that the activities they teach need to be experienced positively in the first place, or conditions need to be provided so that they can be experienced positively. It could also be argued that a focus upon outcomes such as tackling obesity or identifying talent will ultimately create a discourse where these values take precedence. Over time, a restricted rhetoric of health, if constantly extolled by the teachers, could further alienate many individuals from their bodies and reduce potential participation during the lifecourse. Consequently, as well as revealing the complexities of how 'fun' can be experienced, a further aim in writing this book is to promote mechanisms through which sport practitioners can reflect upon their practices and, in particular, think about the ways in which they 'see' sport and how these views may impact upon the children and adults they teach.

The ideas presented in this book are intended to give the reader the opportunity to assess the broader, subjective aspects of sporting experience. While the book sits within the context of a series which focuses on *physical education and youth sport,* examples have been purposefully included in order to explore adult experiences of sport so that reflections upon consequences of earlier experiences can be considered. As James Sallis purports (Sallis and Owen 1999), and is supported through empirical evidence gathered in the research I have been involved in, school-based physical education is often (if not the only) experience of sport for many young people. It has been with this in mind that I have attempted to focus my research lens upon both current and previous experiences of children and adults. It is considered essential to acknowledge the significance of previous experiences of school sport and PE so that consideration can be made about current and future practices. As Kirk rightfully highlights in *Physical Education Futures* (2010), we need to be clearer about what we actually want from PE and the implications that any concrete actions will have upon its future form.

Therefore, my main aim in writing this book is to explore the relevance of embodied fun (in its many forms) and to generate ideas for further discussion relating to its impact upon participation in sport. I begin in Chapter 2 by introducing the theoretical framework for the book. In particular it details the concept of body-reflexive pleasures. The concept is explored through acknowledgement of the broader theoretical influences (Ahmed 2010, Connell 2005, Pronger 2002, Sartre 1954) and by attempting to position these arguments within current approaches to thinking about the body in the context of sport and physical activity.

Chapter 3 explores sporting experiences within the context of school sports and PE and in particular the subjective experiences of children. The chapter explores the notion of wellbeing in terms of the competing adult discourses relating to the perceived benefits for taking part in sport and the subjective experiences of sport for the school children. Central to children's experiences of sport is the notion that the activities should be 'fun', although it is through analysis of what children understand by fun that a more sophisticated interpretation of fun, enjoyment and pleasure can be revealed. The chapter draws upon research conducted in schools as part of a large-scale research project, the National School Sport Week, held in England, Scotland and Wales. This sporting initiative (delivered nationwide through private sponsorship) provided an opportunity for detailed qualitative research which was conducted among a range of children (using drawing activities, recorded conversations and observations). Discussion is centred on the contrasting ways in which the children 'enjoyed' the activities and these were often in sharp contrast to the expected outcomes of the adult sponsors. Examples highlight the centrality of embodied experience for the children as well as the complexities of providing for children's wellbeing.

In Chapters 4, 5 and 6, I adopt a more qualitative approach to exploring the subjectivities at play in the way that individuals experience enjoyment within the activities they engage in. The intention is to provide examples of the processes through which an activity is experienced as fun. Through the application of qualitative interviews and personal reflection, I attempt to reveal further the complexities of fun and enjoyment. In Chapter 4, I explore the role of pleasure as a significant ingredient within the context of large-scale initiatives aimed at children and young people out of school hours. I use examples taken from research conducted as part of two nationwide programmes which were aimed at attracting the 'non-sporty' as well as those in disadvantaged areas. The main focus of this chapter is a community-based sports club aimed at disabled young people which explores the significance of social embodied pleasure as well as the embodied 'resilience' in the face of broader social constructions of those considered appropriate to take part in sport. In this case, attention focuses on the experiences of Jodie and Nick, a disabled participant and a volunteer helper. By giving Jodie and Nick central stage, the intention is to theorise the issues which they felt were important in their lives and to assess these in relation to broader debates about the benefits of participating in sport-based leisure activities. Their 'stories' are followed by further examples drawn from participants in a nationwide programme (providing 'doorstep' sport to young people) to highlight the contrasting ways that young people experience (or are allowed to experience) and enjoy sporting activities aimed specifically at them.

Chapter 5 explores the theme of bodily pleasure in sport participation through empirical research conducted with those often falling 'outside' the traditional focus of the sports provision. In this case, the focus is not elite and professional sports men and women, but rather the 'amateur' sports enthusiast. Interviews (sporting-life histories) are incorporated which focus upon the bodily experiences and pleasure within the context of sport and physical activity. These particular methodological approaches have been utilised successfully in previous research where the intention was to gather material which provides qualitative accounts of experiencing the body in sporting contexts (Wellard 2007, 2009). A series of semi-structured interviews were conducted at differing sites for physical activity and sport between 2009 and 2012. Two examples of middle-aged adults are explored in detail to provide an in-depth account of the pathway to, as well as experience of, swimming and running. Here, participation is primarily a voluntary decision and considered in the light of previous (non-) sporting experiences at school and as young adults. Consequently, the physical and emotional experiences are revealed as well as their displays of resilience.

Chapter 6 incorporates a reflective approach to personal experiences of sport as a means to question further the subjective complexities of individual engagement in physical activity. The intention in this chapter is to provide personal accounts of childhood experience as well as current adult experiences to explore the ways in which consideration of subjective engagement does not necessarily mean isolated, individual acts. Rather, it is more the case that shared stories can reveal similarities in the everyday experiences of the recreational sports participant.

   The final chapter summarises the debates and analysis presented in the book. This summary is used to provoke further discussion on why such discussion is useful to sport (as well as health and body) studies and how these debates fit with existing sport theory. The conclusions suggest that existing theories of the sporting body (and sports participation) evident in sport studies fail to consider fully the relevance of fun and enjoyment or, indeed, embodied pleasure. In this way, the book provides new insights that might help shape future projects and thinking about the sporting body, as well as adult and child participation in sport and general wellbeing.

Note

1 Many of the research projects I have been involved in were sport-related programmes funded by public, private sector and third sector organisations. The initiatives they were sponsoring tended to involve an intervention of some sort, usually where a sport or activities were introduced into a school or community.

2   Theorising sport and *body-reflexive pleasures*

For a period in my childhood, I lived in South Australia. Our family had a house right next to the sea in a small town south of Adelaide. The house was about 100 metres away from a long sandy beach which was interrupted by the mouth of a river. The river separated the beach with about 25 metres of fast-flowing water pouring into the ocean. For a child in early adolescence, our house provided access to a natural adventure playground with unlimited possibilities. It was always a great thrill to swim across the river mouth as the current was strong and made swimming a little more challenging. However, the biggest thrill for me was found at the rocks which formed the border of the river mouth to the land. The rocks were on one side of the river, while on the other side there were sand dunes where one could slide down into the water. The rocks were exciting because they provided the opportunity at the point where the river met the sea to climb up them and jump into the water below. The ledge from where it was possible to jump was only about 4 or 5 metres above the water, but it felt like jumping off a mountain. At this point the water was also quite deep which made it feel like one was plummeting to the bottom of the sea on entry. This was followed by a mad scramble to get back to the surface. Another thrill in this adventure was the awareness that there were sharks in the sea. There were often newspaper reports about attacks on surfers at nearby beaches, but this knowledge did not put us off as the thrill of throwing oneself from the ledge into the deep water below was too enticing. My group of friends had reasoned that if there was a shark below, we would probably stun it when we jumped on it, so we would have time to get to out of the water if need be.

(A personal reflection upon a childhood experience)

Frank lunged through the crowded bath at him. Maurice and me joined him, the others shot out. He screamed for help. We got hold of the wild animal and shoved his obscene head under the cold water tap. Maurice tickled his ribs. Water cascaded into the dressing room. Everybody joined the shrieking. Arnie was tortured with his own laughter.

(David Storey, *This Sporting Life*)

Taking part in a sporting activity involves a range of physical and emotional sensations which are interwoven with the individual body as well as the social context in which the experience occurs. Physical and mental states overlap and work together and, although a particular sensation, whether physical or psychological, may be the focus of the experience as it happens, the build up to and subsequent reflection generate a broader understanding which can be either positive or negative. Engaging in a sporting activity is, therefore, part of a 'whole package' (Wellard 2002) and requires a complex range of social relationships both on and off the field of play.

My personal reflection and the extract from *This Sporting Life*, above, reveal some of the aspects of sporting activity that are enjoyable but not necessarily directly related to the specific sport, such as, in these cases, swimming and rugby. Indeed, as Storey details in his fictional account of working-class rugby players, the embodied, physical relationships with other men at the club (teammates, opponents, management) were central to the protagonist's experiences of – among other things – pleasure, pain, pride and shame. For the central character, pleasure was most noticeably gained through embodied experiences with his teammates after the game in the form of camaraderie, intimacy, physical play and a sense of belonging. In both examples, the social aspect of 'being' with others enhanced the experiences of jumping into the sea water or the physical horseplay in the communal bath after the match. The significance of fun and a play element in both cases also suggests a greater connection between what are often considered contrasting contexts of childhood play and adult sport.

My aim for writing this book is to explore the processes through which a sporting activity is experienced, in an attempt to account qualitatively for the multitude of individual and external influences which determine whether participation is considered pleasurable or not. In doing so, I attempt to incorporate a personal and reflexive approach within the research process in order to consider further some of the issues relating to embodiment and physical activity which still remain uncharted. Themes around physical pleasure, fun and enjoyment as factors in sporting participation appeared constantly in the narratives of interviews conducted during previous research with children and adults (Wellard 2009). However, as is the case in much sociological research, although I was able to produce rich data during the fieldwork, I felt that at times I was somehow 'hiding' behind the research. Using interviews had allowed me to explore questions that I had been considering in relation to the ways in which others developed understandings of their own bodies and sporting performance. Particularly in relation to my research with adults, listening to the voices of other men helped allay fears that the ideas I had were not isolated but the result of socially informed 'shared' knowledge. There were occasions when it might have been illuminating to incorporate my own thoughts and feelings more. Indeed, it was often when reading through my personal field notes that I was more able to critically unpack my initial research questions and put them into more perspective. While making attempts to reconcile individual experiences with social relationships is hardly new, I have always wanted to promote the virtues of extending the limits of conventional theoretical thinking, particularly in the way that Pronger (2002) describes the 'philosophy of limit' where boundaries are set which restrict possibilities for exploring beyond them.

This chapter considers the theory underpinning the ideas put forward in this book. In particular it details the concept of body-reflexive pleasures, which will be explored through acknowledgement of the broader theoretical influences as well as an attempt to position this within current approaches to thinking about the body in the context of sport and physical activity.

At this stage, however, it is worthwhile to consider the recent appropriation of 'wellbeing' by a range of disparate interested parties (academics, politicians, health educators, sport practitioners and so on). The interest in wellbeing relates to both children and adults and has more recently become a justification for making objective assumptions about 'what is good for' individuals and groups of individuals. An interesting and possibly more useful way of thinking about wellbeing can be seen in Vernon's (2008) suggestion that the concept of wellbeing derives more from happiness where it follows that happiness and pleasure are inextricably linked. Indeed, it is difficult to define wellbeing without taking into account the complexities of understanding pleasure.

Part of the problem is the continued dovetailing of terms such as fun, enjoyment, pleasure and happiness and the subsequent failure to fully interpret their meanings within the context of an overall sporting experience. Although I am not setting out to establish or provide specific classifications for these terms, what I am suggesting is that it is important to reveal the complex ways that these embodied sensations are experienced at the subjective level precisely because simplistic and narrow descriptions invariably allow other ways of experiencing (or benefitting from) sporting activities (such as physical fitness, skills acquisition, discipline and competition) to take precedence without fully considering the consequences.

It may be relatively easy to talk of physical fitness levels in more objective terms, but concepts such as fun or wellbeing are less obvious. Recent post-structuralist explanations of the discourses surrounding social formulations of 'physical fitness', have demonstrated that they are still understood more readily within a scientific framework (Pronger 2002). If we consider wellbeing in terms of philosophical understanding, we are drawn into the ontological assessment of an individual state of being. In this case, wellbeing is often contemplated in terms of individual pleasure and states of happiness. Mark Vernon (2008) attempts to look at the meaning beyond the actual or intrinsic feeling of pleasure and suggests that although wellbeing derives from happiness, it is less subjective. In a similar manner to the contemplation of happiness, most of the questions relating to it are framed in terms of 'how we achieve it'. As Vernon suggests, part of the modern day obsession with finding happiness is influenced heavily by consumerist discourses:

> Keeping up with the Joneses is what you come to love because it secretly gives you more pleasure – maybe more than a rising standard of living does

itself. Hence, in a market place of easy, pleasurable luxuries, unhappiness will spread.

(Vernon 2008: 23)

Graham (1995) noted how the business model of 'consumer choice' was being applied to American schools in the latter stages of the twentieth century. This approach opened up debate about the notion of 'listening' to student voices in the context of them being customers. The notion of considering a student in terms of a 'happy' customer created uneasy tensions with existing philosophies within education and healthcare where the decisions practitioners were making were ultimately 'for the good' of their students or patients. Graham's ideas were generated during a time when there was much work produced on the effects of consumer lifestyles (for example, Bourdieu 1986, Urry 1995, Featherstone *et al.* 1991, Tomlinson 1990), the notion that individual happiness or wellbeing has been shaped through a quest to 'keep up with the Joneses' reflects a contemporary formulation of what is required to achieve a perceived ideal state of being. But this very much incorporates a socio-cultural perspective and how our relationships with others affect perceived states of happiness or wellbeing.

The influence of the social is evidenced in Ereaut and Whiting's (2008) research into the ways in which wellbeing is defined and interpreted within an English government department and highlights the contrasting ways in which it is understood. They attempt to offer ways in which it can (or should) be understood in order to maintain consistency.

> We would suggest that the first and most important way to make sense of how 'wellbeing' behaves in contemporary discourse is this: wellbeing is a *social construct*. There are no uncontested biological, spiritual, social, economic or any other kind of markers for wellbeing. The meaning of wellbeing is not fixed – it cannot be. It is a *primary cultural judgement*; just like *'what makes a good life?'* it is the stuff of fundamental philosophical debate. What it means at any one time depends on the weight given at that time to different philosophical traditions, world views and systems of knowledge. How far any one view dominates will determine how stable its meaning is, so its meaning will always be shifting, though maybe more at some times than others.

(Ereaut and Whiting 2008: 9)

The researchers found that for many of the respondents 'wellbeing' was not a familiar term and it was difficult to apply the concept in a context which readily appealed to personal sentiments. In most cases, when pressed, the respondents offered interpretations which related to health and access to basic provisions considered necessary for a reasonable standard of living, such as food, water and housing. To an extent, they were applying descriptions similar to indicators of poverty, which itself has been constantly reassessed (Dornan *et al.* 2004, Alcock 2006).

However, a central issue which helps unified thinking about standards of living is its relationship to economics. In the case of wellbeing, Ereaut and Whiting (2008) found that what could be considered an apparently central issue in a government department's strategy was not uniformly understood. Much of this ambiguity related to age-old debates of theory and practice. Whereas an issue like poverty, although open to theoretical debate as a concept, can be addressed in terms of economic measures to 'reduce' levels and increase overall standards of living, in the case of wellbeing the philosophical visions do not sit so easily with the operational requirements, particularly in the way it can be measured. As Ereaut and Whiting suggest,

> While a useful template, and essential tool for business-as-usual, the opera-tionalised definition will never *fully* represent the broad ambition. It cannot, in that it does not fully meet wider societal understanding of wellbeing, and perhaps was never intended to.
>
> (Ereaut and Whiting 2008:19)

Within the context of the research process, rather than attempting to gauge the wellbeing 'levels' of individuals, it is more fruitful to incorporate research methodologies which can develop an understanding of, for example, how participation in a specific intervention is experienced as 'enjoyable' as well as health-enhancing and contributing to wellbeing. For instance, the focus for research would be collecting data which could assist in generating understanding of the individual's lived experience of the intervention within the immediate context of their lived social environment.

Consequently, claims that measures are being introduced in order to achieve 'wellbeing' for targeted groups of individuals (as a specific outcome) become less convincing. This is particularly so in the case of many young people and adults with limited previous experience or enthusiasm for sport. The broader, and arguably more significant, embodied pleasurable aspects to be found in sport and physical activity are often overlooked in favour of specific health-related measures. The implication is that the motivation for taking part is, for example, to lose weight, with the consequence that an individual's introduction (and subsequent orientation) to sport and physical activity is restricted to a specific outcome, rather than as an enjoyable embodied experience. It could be claimed that in physical education (PE) and school sports, the physical body is further 'disembodied' (Evans *et al.* 2004) through focus upon health-based 'outcomes' and what could be considered a 'fear of fun' which cannot be accounted for in the objective forms prescribed by government directives. Much of this 'fear' of fun is developed through misplaced association of fun with hedonism, where this narrow version is shaped through heteronormative understandings of adult sexual behaviour.

However, fun, enjoyment and pleasure do not necessarily have to be selfish and hedonistic and, ultimately, it could be claimed that undue focus solely upon psychological 'wellbeing' and outcome-driven curriculum policy restricts the potential for individual accomplishment and learning about the possibilities of the physical body. Thus it is argued that pleasurable physical feelings are experienced at both the individual and the social level, at a specific time as well as in a later positive (or negative) reflection.

Sport, fun and pleasure

When you are backing up someone who has made a break and in a split second, before you've had time to think, you cut inside, the ball pops up right in front of you, and the whole thing rolls on in a blur with other players backing up .... You live for these moments.

(Willy, quoted in Pringle 2009: 221)

The lip held long enough for me to rise to my feet and dig the rail of the board into the wall before it collapsed onto the reef below; somehow, I stayed in front of the crashing thunder for the next twenty seconds. At the edge of the reef I safely glided out of the exhausted slab; at this moment a surge of endorphins flushed my body engulfing me in euphoria.

(Booth 2009: 133)

From an early age I felt, I felt sort of aware, maybe not sexually, but sensu-ously, you know, my body and sort of stimulating my body. I mean to say when we used to climb ropes in gym and obviously our legs were wrapped around them, I think I can remember getting a frisson of excitement... but I didn't know what it was, I just got the, you know, the very sort of warm feeling about. We all do when we're children, by accident in some ways, something you found, a new area of sensation. I think I did that... it's funny how it's sort of associated with climbing ropes, gym work and things like that, sport actually does make you more aware of that.

(Keith, 46, quoted in Wellard 2009: 141)

The different experiences described by Willy, Douglas Booth and Keith highlight a range of factors: the sensual feelings of the body in movement, the thrill of the body confronting natural elements and the excitement of the physical body with other bodies in the context of a (constructed) social event such as rugby. What is important is that all of these experiences are noted and remembered, which in turn shapes future anticipation. Willy states that these are moments he lives for, which suggests that they are a significant reason for his continued participation. Similarly, the euphoria which Booth describes and the sensuality that Keith felt were justifications for wanting to take part in physical activities again. This was particularly the case with Keith, whom I interviewed as part of my research into masculinities and the sporting body (Wellard 2009). Keith, possibly in contrast to the others, did not have a conventional path through school sport and did not feel comfortable taking part in sport until well into adulthood. However, the memories of those initial enjoyable experiences provided the motivation to return as an adult, when participation could be negotiated in more favourable ways.

There has been limited academic debate exploring the notion of pleasure in sport and it has tended to focus upon the spectator (Guttmann 1996) whereby pleasure is derived through the erotic gaze, or as a form of hedonistic gratification (McNamee 2005, Bloodworth *et al.* 2012). The alignment of pleasure with the erotic can be seen to provide one explanation as to why pleasure (and in consequence fun) is considered problematic as attempts to promote the moral values of sport (particularly within school settings) do not rest easily alongside the traditional interpretations of pleasure equated with the erotic or sexual. However, there has been more recently an attempt to account for the broader experience of pleasure in sport and along with it a greater awareness of the multifaceted and complex ways in which it is understood, such as the physiological experience of endorphins (Booth 2009), the ambiguity of violence, pleasure and pain (Pringle 2009, Pickard 2007) and moments of pleasure (Wellard 2012).

The example of Keith, above, was taken from research conducted with a range of amateur sportsmen (Wellard 2009). Keith reflected upon his experiences of school sport (in this case climbing bars in gymnastics) and talked about a sensuousness that he found in these bodily movements which for all intents could be considered erotic experiences. Another interviewee (Angus) in the same research talked about his experiences, as a teenager, in the school changing rooms where having an erection in the showers (after playing rugby) was an 'event' that was a physical thrill as well as a source of humour among his classmates rather than that of shame and embarrassment. In each case, it could be claimed that the understandings of pleasure have been drawn from beyond the boundaries of conventional thinking about how and when pleasure occurs in the context of sport. Incorporating embodied experience and the erotic in such accounts, although at face value highly subjective, demonstrates that broader definitions rely on both individual and social interpretations of pleasure and erotic experience. However, the sensuousness that Keith describes during his embodied experience of the gymnastics lessons is not accounted for in conventional thinking about the sensuous body, in the same way that the embodied intimacy shared by David Storey's rugby players in the communal bath cannot be explained sufficiently through heteronormative interpretations of sexual pleasure. These experiences were, indeed, 'sexy' but not in the limited descriptions available in heteronormative discourse (Butler 1993). As Michael Atkinson describes in his accounts of fell running, the existential, embodied feelings are hard to fully articulate within the discourses available to us.

> *I did my first 10-mile, Category A fell run this morning. No words fight now, I'll have to write about it in detail later tonight or tomorrow when I can focus. My mind is gone, my legs shattered. We head out to do the same run tomorrow, and I cannot wait. The juxtaposition between the beauty of the fell and the existential ordeal generated by running is almost too intense to put into words, almost like raucous sex with the hills.*
>
> (Atkinson 2010: 127)

A more critical, embodied understanding of how sport can be experienced is not easily expressed with conventional interpretations of 'sex'. However, by exploring the intense subjective experiences, like the ones that Atkinson describes, there is the potential to think beyond the boundaries. Nevertheless, sport continues to provide a variety of erotica because of the way the body is central to the activity and the spectacle and how bodily movements are demonstrated. It is not only the corporeality of sport that can be considered erotic; the narratives of sporting contest are also open to erotic interpretation. Taken this way, the erotic is about a sense of liberation in relation to sexual expression; it is about celebrating the sensuality of sexual desire and the pleasures of sexual excitement. Ultimately, it is often the case that within the context of sport, the possibilities which arise to challenge established understandings of gender, sexuality and bodily experience can be lost in the effort to adopt or adapt to the (hetero)normative performances of mainstream sport. Pronger (2002) describes how these social constructions place limits on the way we contemplate the body and impede the potential, or 'puissance' (2002: 66), to be found in bodily pleasures that exist 'outside' the boundaries of conventional thinking. Recognition of the erotic highlights ways in which sexuality is experienced by individuals, either physically or emotionally (through the senses) as well as being a guiding factor in the social organization of many individuals through formulations of appropriate outlets for or manifestations of sexual desire.

Investigation of the way in which sexual desire is organised in contemporary society reveals, in fact, the limited ways in which sex, sexual relations and our understanding of the physical and emotional body are constructed and enacted within 'western' discourse. Much of this limited understanding derives from biological explanations of heteronormative sex based on a dualist notion of male and female roles within a penetration/reproduction relationship (Firestone 1979, Petchesky 1986, Dimen 2003) as well as historical, social constructions of the body (Foucault 1976, Shilling 1993, Synnott 1993). Indeed, it could be claimed that such narrow thinking has contributed to a fear of pleasure in social and private spaces because of the association of pleasure with hedonism and promiscuous sexual activity.

Sex when associated with sport is mostly considered in terms of spectatorship where sporty bodies are consumed by adoring fans (Guttmann 1996, Miller 2001). There is little work that explores the physical pleasure of sporting activity in a corporeal sense. Pronger (1990) talks about the erotic aspects of the sports locker room, but this is as a way of decoding sexual gaze and the ironies of the mythologised gym as a sanctuary for heterosexual masculinity. The ontological aspects of 'being' in the context of sport and physical activities are less documented. It may be simple to declare that an element of participation was 'fun' or 'sexy' but fully accounting for that feeling as an emotional, social *and* physical experience is more complex. Nevertheless, it is important not to make distinctions but rather incorporate theory that can accommodate the plethora of competing emotions and sensations.

Just as Pringle (2009) identifies how the correlation of violence with pleasure is complex, what is understood as erotic has shifted according to history and culture. For instance, a statue of Eros was common in the *palaestrae* or Greek wrestling schools for men. Here the statue embodied erotic love of men and passion for males and male bodies. Rowe (1999) makes the point, citing the work of Guttmann (1996), that it is impossible to ignore the historical linkage of sport and the erotic because of how the body appears in sporting participation and sports contests. Greek wrestlers can be understood as providing male sensual expression through toned bodies and athletic movement, which are arousing and exciting, and therefore erotic. However, we no longer see statues of Eros in men's wrestling arenas as there has been a shift in what is understood as erotic for men or what is considered socially acceptable for public display.

I have specifically included the reference to the erotic and western understanding of the sexual body as this clearly has an impact on the ways in which fun and enjoyment in sport are considered. There is often confusion in the way that fun is classified in relation to children's play when associated with school-based sport and young people. Or, it is associated with pleasure within the context of adult sport. In this case, the narrow understanding of pleasure constructs fun as something that is trivial, non-serious and ultimately too subjective. However, the ways in which children and adults use 'fun' as a description of their experience of an activity demands further unpacking rather than an assumption that it is meaningless. Fun, within the context of the arguments expressed in this book, is considered to be an 'umbrella' term that incorporates a wide variety of physical, psychological and social experiences. Subjective accounts of fun are not necessarily solipsistic in that they operate in terms of purely selfish motivations. Revealing the multiple ways in which fun is an integral part of a sporting activity can help us understand participation.

For example, Sport England recently conducted a large-scale quantitative study into the sporting participation levels of people aged over 19 in England[1]. The intention was to gain a fuller understanding of the extent to which people are participating (or not) in sport in an attempt to develop strategies to get more people actively involved in sport. The study incorporated a national telephone survey (the Active People Survey) where questions were asked about recent participation and levels of activity. The survey data was used to compile a series of profiles or 'market segments' of typical groups of sports participants.

The study was proclaimed as one of the first major investigations into sporting participation in England and, although the data was clearly useful in many contexts, the subsequent analysis and conclusions drawn from it were ultimately misleading. Part of the problem was an attempt to pigeon-hole specific groups of people into categories that could be targeted for specific actions. The 'market' approach to identifying 'segments' within society incorporated similar practices to those used within advertising and marketing and attempted to focus the analysis on the formation of simplistic generalisations that could be readily targeted by sport deliverers to potential sporting consumers.

The failure to fully understand the complexities of participation can be seen in the way that issues about 'what drives participation' were considered by asking a simple question such as 'What is your main motivation for taking part in sport?' For this question, eight possible answers were offered:

Just enjoy it	*Keep fit*	*Meet with friends*	*Take children*
Help with injury/ disability	*Lose weight*	*Improve performance*	*Competition*

'Just enjoy it' was the most highly rated response in 14 of the 19 segments. In these categories, 'Keep fit' was rated second. In the five other categories, Keep fit was rated first while Just enjoy it was rated second. However, there was no account taken of the way in which enjoyment was experienced, or explanations offered as to why enjoyment might have been the main motivation. Clearly, enjoyment was a factor, but it appeared difficult for those analysing the data to make connections between the competing ways in which enjoyment might be experienced and the extent to which the other factors (such as meeting friends or competition) might have been a significant factor in the enjoyment.

Body-reflexive pleasures

Although discussion of the body has been incorporated within many recent explorations of sport and PE (Evans *et al.* 2004, Gard and Wright 2005, Maivorsdotter and Lundvall 2009) the corporeal aspects (or the nitty-gritty elements of the 'lived' body) which ultimately influence the way an individual develops a sense of their own identity are not always fully accounted for. So, whereas the discursive structures operating upon the body revealed by Foucauldian and many post-structuralist accounts (such as Butler 1993) have been extensively debated, there does seem room for more discussion about embodied experience. In particular, the ways in which individuals create corporeal understandings of their own bodies and in turn develop understandings of their own physical identities as well as others.

There has, however, been a notable interest in the meaning and experience of movement within the context of physical education, which could be described as a phenomenology of movement (Smith 2007). Much of the focus here is to address the perceived lack of understanding about the qualities and characteristics of movement among physical education practitioners. As Brown and Payne suggest,

> Repositioning the phenomenology of movement within the discourse of physical education, and making claims about the meaningful nature of the experience of movement inevitably confronts problems and challenges about how various aspects of the discourse of physical education and its research have historically, culturally and ecologically been conceptualized, contextualised, represented, and legitimised.
>
> (Brown and Payne 2009: 418)

The concept of a 'phenomenology of movement' is undoubtedly a significant influence in the way I am exploring the experience of fun and enjoyment. However, I have also been drawn to theoretical positions which acknowledge the role of the body in shaping external social practices. As such, the concept of body-reflexive practices (Connell (2005) has been incorporated (for reasons which will become apparent) within this context, as this enables the application of a social constructionist approach which incorporates the physical body within these social processes. As Connell suggests,

> Bodies, in their own right as bodies, do matter. They age, get sick, enjoy, engender, give birth. There is an irreducible bodily dimension in experience and practice: the sweat cannot be excluded.
>
> (Connell 2005: 51).

Obviously, there are discourses which seek to explain social understandings of areas such as bodily health and sickness, but all too often they do not take into account the individual, corporeal experience of the body. Maybe there are fears of moving towards biological essentialism, but this need not be the case. I have described elsewhere (Wellard 2006b, 2009) how my enjoyment of sporting and physical activities has often been compromised by the requirements to manage and negotiate my body (particularly in relation to performances of hegemonic masculinity) in socially expected ways. I am not alone in this, as the potential bodily pleasures experienced through sporting activity have to be managed within social understandings of a range of discourses, such as gender, sexuality, age and ability, which may ultimately, prevent or diminish my ability or willingness to take part. It is here that Connell's arguments have resonance, as they form the basis of an understanding of the importance of the social and physical body and bodily practices. Connell attempts to incorporate the role of the biological (in this case, in the social construction of gender) and also applies a sociological reading of the social world where social factors are exposed to the restrictions created by social structures. She explains that

> With bodies both objects and agents of practice, and the practice itself forming the structures within which bodies are appropriated and defined, we face a pattern beyond the formulae of current social theory. This pattern might be termed body-reflexive practice.
>
> (Connell 2005: 61)

Body-reflexive practices are, she argues, formed through a circuit of bodily experiences which link to bodily interaction and bodily experience via socially constructed bodily understandings which lead to new bodily interactions. As a result, Connell argues that social theory needs to account for the corporeality of the body. It is 'through body-reflexive practices, bodies are addressed by social process and drawn into history, without ceasing to be bodies... they do not turn into symbols, signs or positions in discourse' (2005: 64).

Connell's concept of body-reflexive practices helps us understand how social and cultural factors interact with individual experiences of the body. This in turns creates a need to recognise not only the social forms and practices which underpin the individual's ability to take part in sport, or any other physical activity, but also the unique experiences or physical thrill of bodily based expression.

Consequently, it seems worthwhile to adapt the concept in order to incorporate a circuit of *body-reflexive pleasures*, located within the context of the body, sport and physical activities. Indeed, it is within this context that it is equally important to recognise the range of factors which contribute to the experience of pleasure (or not). Thus if we apply the concept to an individual's experience of a sport we can see that consideration needs to be made of the social, physiological and psychological processes that occur at any level and with varied influence. Pleasure is therefore central as part of a circuit of interconnected factors which determine the individual experience. Figure 2.1, below, illustrates that a circuit of events is constantly being experienced and negotiated, resulting in either a positive or negative orientation towards sport and physical activity.

All three dimensions contribute, at different levels, to the overall experience of the activity, rendering it either positive or negative. Consequently, demarcating pleasure to merely represent a subjective, intrinsic moment fails to take into account the range of competing factors which influence the experience. Thus, pleasure understood within this concept is more than a one-off moment of individual gratification, but rather a process whereby the pleasurable experience contributes to contemplation before and after the moment in the form of anticipation and reflection. The ways in which these dimensions relate to an individual experience can be further explained by looking at each one in more detail.

Social context

Psychological experience or feeling

Physiological experience

Figure 2.1 Circuit of body-reflexive pleasure

Psychological contexts

Much of the research within sport that has acknowledged fun and pleasure has tended to focus on psychological performance in relation to being in the 'zone', such as the way Csikszentmihalyi (1990) describes 'Flow'. However, too often these approaches are quick to disassociate elements of pleasure as an insignificant part of the process and do not fully account for the contribution of the physiological and the social elements. Alternatively, the contribution of fun or enjoyment is acknowledged as a (minor) factor in motivation towards taking part in physical activity, such as in the example provided above relating to Sport England's 'market segment' approach. Particularly in the context of motivation as a factor in participation, the focus on health behaviours can be seen in the development of 'models' of sporting participation such as the transtheoretical model (Prochaska and DiClemente 2005) and the theory of self-determination (Deci and Ryan 2000).

The transtheoretical model has been widely incorporated in health planning and, in particular, the focus upon its application to exercise behaviour has generated broader debate (Hagger and Chatzisarantis 2009). At the heart of this model is the belief that behaviour change within an individual occurs along a sequence of stages, each with distinct psycho-social traits and patterns and behaviour variables (Hagger and Chatzisarantis, 2005). The theory of self-determination can be viewed as a contemporary theory of motivation where the recognition of innate psychological needs is required (Deci and Ryan 2000). The theory assumes the presence of three inherent and essential psychological needs requiring fulfilment, which coordinate human motivation: self-determination, competitiveness and relatedness (Deci and Ryan 2000, Chatzisarantis *et al.* 2002). These needs exist as personal requirements for the individual to act as a self-initiator and regulator in order to achieve behavioural outcomes and gain fulfilment from relationships with significant others. It is argued that such needs are crucial for the development of the self, psychologically and physically, and specifically in the nurturing of motivation and sustaining of wellbeing (Chatzisarantis *et al.* 2002).

The problem with these models, as well as in the proliferation of subsequent variations, is that, apart from focusing solely on the psychological 'motivations' for taking part in physical activity, they tend to compartmentalise 'types' of behaviour and isolate 'stages' of behaviour. Nevertheless, these theories have become popular with government agencies, keen to find overarching models that can be incorporated into toolkits that can respond to perceived shortfalls in physical activity participation. In doing so, much of the focus becomes about looking at barriers to participation with the presumption that behaviour changes move in one direction and that, once barriers have been removed, the experience of the activity will be enjoyed.

Another way to think about the psychological factors that play heavily on our experience of sport is through consideration of what makes an activity less pleasurable. Often, a reason for not enjoying or not wanting to take part in an activity is fear of letting oneself down in some way. Shame, therefore, provides a useful contrast to notions of wellbeing and 'happiness' that are considered as expected outcomes once barriers have been removed and participation has been achieved. Whereas we might consider happiness to be something that we all strive for in certain ways, the notion of shame is something that might be considered as detrimental to happiness.

Elspeth Probyn (2005) describes the complex relationship of shame to joy and enjoyment. As a starting point, she uses the work of the psychologist Silvan Tompkins to show how shame emerges after interest or enjoyment has been activated. Probyn's argument is that we need to recognise shame as a factor that explains or describes how something is enjoyed. Consequently, exploring shame is one way to explain further the complexities of enjoyment. For instance, we can feel shameful about enjoying something at all, or even too much, such as eating an extra slice of chocolate cake. Our taste buds may tell us it is delicious, whereas our social conscience (knowledge acquired through social discourses related to health, body cultures and greed)warns us about consequences of eating excessive calories. This perspective raises interesting questions about the assumptions made in sport and physical education that being 'good at' is not necessarily coterminous with enjoying it. For it may be the case that ability can bring with it a feeling of shame associated with being 'too good' and subsequent feelings of alienation.

However, within the context of taking part in sport, the centrality of performance, particularly in team games, presents a more constant threat of 'letting the side down'. For example, in my study of the gendered 'performances' during mixed social club sessions at an English tennis club, I noted the following:

During these social tennis sessions, there was a concerted effort to 'balance' the games so that more able players, in terms of their tennis ability were not matched against less skilled players. This was achieved either by selecting mixed sex teams or balancing good players with 'weaker' ones. It was interesting that all members appeared to learn their position within the hierarchy of playing ability and there appeared little dissent. However, the attempts to balance the play on closer observation did not always conform solely to playing ability. In many ways the structure favoured the adult male players who were under the age of fifty. The next in line were the elderly men, followed by women and juniors. The men who played in the A team were considered the highest standard followed by the men's B team (the elderly men formed the mainstay of the B team). The women's A team was next, although there were two women who were able to play at a higher standard than most of the men in the B team. Consequently, most status was afforded to the men in the A team. This was continually acknowledged in the selection process for games when pairs were decided. I often heard, 'You're much too good for us', or 'You can take the three of us on by yourself' to an extent that some of the weaker players openly expressed embarrassment based on the belief that they would not be able to compete at the same level and 'let the side down'. Often when there was an uneven balance of men and women, some of the 'weaker' male players assumed the 'female' role in the pair.

Often this happened in small internal, social tournaments when there were usually more men. The role was generally adopted without any complaint, but usually accompanied by some form of humour.

(Wellard 2009: 43)

If read in terms of an activity that catered for a mix of gender, age and ability, the tennis sessions described clearly tick the boxes. However, closer examination of the processes and social rituals that shaped how the tennis was allowed to be played ultimately affected the experiences of the individuals taking part in contrasting ways. The levels of enjoyment and shame were far less uniform and it could not be assumed that the experience of 'playing' tennis was the same for each participant. However, what is important in making sense of this example is that it can be assumed that the participants had played tennis before and had had time to negotiate their position within the club and make assessments of the ways in which they participated and enjoyed their participation. In contrast to the psychological models described earlier which tend to focus upon the barriers to entering into sporting participation, it is clearly the case that experiences once 'in' are equally significant.

For Probyn, shame provides the opportunity to reflect upon and assess how it 'compels an involuntary and immediate reassessment of ourselves' (2005: xii). Revealing and disclosing shame, according to Probyn, tells us about ourselves as well as the social.

The promiscuity of shame, heightened through its telling, broadens notions of what is personal and what is social. The body is key here because it generates and carries so much meaning and in ways that academics have not really attended to. We have tended to over-privilege the body's cultural meanings and have not really tried to tell the psychosomatic body's stories.

(Probyn 2005: 41)

Shame is therefore an internalisation of perceived appropriate behaviour through a continuous interaction and negotiation of the social world. It is not just a psychological condition, but an embodied reaction to the social, which can be manifested through, as Probyn explains, a physical reaction such as blushing. However, other physiological presentations, such as sweating, palpitations and nausea can equally be seen to occur. Consequently, shame can be considered a 'fine line border between moving forward into more interest or falling back into humiliation' (2005: xii). Needless to say, the arguments that Probyn makes resonate strongly with individual experiences of sport and highlight the importance of recognising the broader dynamics of embodied experience.

The question of why something is humiliating is one way of understanding how an activity is enjoyable or not. Importantly, and in a similar manner to Connell (2005), Probyn acknowledges the influence of the biological. She claims that shame is biologically innate as 'we are all born with the capacity for shame' (2005: xiii). From my sociological standpoint, and one which resonates with

Probyn, I find this position appealing in that it allows consideration of the way in which human beings are similar rather than different and thus allows opportunity for the incorporation of a broader inclusion agenda.

Physiological contexts

Booth (2009), drawing upon Caillois' concept of *ilinx*, describes 'moments' of pleasure which cause a temporary destruction or disruption of the stability of perception. In this case, Booth describes his experiences of surfing, which some may consider falls into the category of 'extreme' sports. However, what Booth does note is the absence of references to pleasure in scholarly works. Although Booth may be accused of adopting a 'thrill seeking' approach to the pursuit of sport, what this highlights is the importance of thinking about the broader dimensions of pleasure and the need to consider not just the biological aspects but also 'the interactions between its biological and sociological components' (Booth 2009: 135).

However, as Pringle (2009) suggests, in the context of sport, there is the tendency to focus upon excitement and thrill which is more often associated with dangerous or deviant activities. Pringle explores the traditional sport of rugby in order to apply a Foucauldian reading of pleasure through, in this case, violence. Consequently, he is able to reveal the complexities of pleasure and the inadequacies of simplistic pain/pleasure dichotomies in explaining the motivations of the rugby players. For many of the players, violence and physical pain were understood in terms of pleasurable experiences. Similarly, Pickard (2007) highlights in her study of young ballet dancers the blurring of pleasure and pain, where in some cases the dancers learned to experience pain as a positive aspect of their development in this field. Thus, in both cases, the social context played a significant part in the way in which the rugby players and dancers learned how to experience their bodies, in contrast to more conventional understandings.

Pickard conducted empirical research with young female ballet dancers to highlight the prevalence of pain and the socially constructed techniques employed by the dancers to negotiate and hide it from the audience. For Pickard, while the body is a central factor in the construction of identities, at a social level of understanding the ballet body is constructed in a binary opposition to a (male) sporting body. However, like men who play sport, negotiating pain increasingly becomes a central focus in the dancers' everyday lives, although the ways the young dancers do this provides sharp contrast to, for example, male boxers or rugby players. Pickard's research, therefore, provides the opportunity to critically assess general assumptions about gender and active participation in physical activities.

In particular, Pickard demonstrates that the girls in her study developed a 'zatopekian' understanding of pain in that they were able to learn to distinguish 'types' of pain that were either positive or negative. For example, one of the young dancers Pickard interviewed described how she understood pain and was planning to increase her pain threshold:

Sometimes my body gets so tired and it aches and I think 'I'll never do anymore' but I do and I feel good. You have to find the determination to do the best you can, you want to prove yourself all the time, to push all the time, sometimes a little 'cos you're scared about how much it is going to hurt but you realise there's more there and it's ok. You might be stiff but you know eventually it'll wear off. You push through it and gain that much more.

(Lie, aged 14, in Pickard 2007)

Pickard draws upon the concepts of positive pain and zatopekian pain to highlight the different ways that pain can be contextualised, and her work presents interesting parallels with other aspects of sport and physical activity training where physical pain is expected and considered an essential part of performance progress. These forms of orientation for thinking about the body have permeated amateur sports and the broader health and fitness industry, for instance in the motivational aspects of fitness training such as 'go for the burn' or 'no pain, no gain'. Consequently, a more complex relationship with pleasure and physical pain is at hand in that physical pain is rearticulated by the individual so that experience of it can be re-evaluated in a more positive, indeed pleasurable, way; for instance, in the way that a charity marathon runner may be able to reflect upon the physical agony of running 26 miles where the pain is considered positively in terms of an indication of effort or achievement (see Elizabeth in Chapter 5). However, in the same way that a boxer may learn to expect pain as part of the whole package of boxing, there are still elements of pleasure in the thrill of anticipation and knowledge that there is a possibility of pain. There may become a contributory factor in the overall assessment of an experience as pleasurable in the way that pain has been avoided where there was a possibility throughout that it could occur, such as a gymnast missing a landing, a miscued rugby tackle or being hit by the ball in dodgeball (see Luke in Chapter 3).

Social contexts

In Chapter 1, I described the enjoyment I experienced during my weekly visits to the public swimming pool. Whereas my love of swimming remains, and as much as I would still love to do a massive bomb in the pool, my social awareness of how a middle-aged man should behave within the context of a social space that is recognised as a *public swimming pool* guides me otherwise. The restrictions that I now feel imposed on my body were less evident as a child as I had no reason to contemplate my social body in terms of it possibly prohibiting participation, or, indeed, as a body that did not belong in the pool. I was part of a world of childhood (Jenks 2005) where physical activity, movement and play are accepted (if not demanded) for able-bodied boys (Kehler and Atkinson 2010). However, as an adult living in a modern 'western' country, I am constantly aware of how the body can (or should) be displayed (Synnott 1993). Consequently, my potential for pleasure is restricted by the social dictates of how a (particular) body should perform in particular spaces. To an extent, a visit to the local pool becomes much more problematic as a lone, middle-aged adult (male) because of the multiple ways in which my presence may be read. The social very much determines the way in which I am able to present my body and in doing so, I need to be constantly aware of how I should be presenting it.

For example, in the UK in 2009, a large leisure and amusement park announced that it was banning men from wearing 'Speedos' in their water-park areas. It was suggested by the management that the small swimming trunks were an affront to public decency and that the predominantly 'family orientated' focus of the theme park was not an appropriate environment for overt displays of male flesh. Investigation of attitudes to displays of the body in contemporary society reveals, in fact, the limited ways in which sex, sexual relations and our understanding of the physical and emotional body are constructed and enacted within 'western' discourse.

The social context of how an apparently innocuous activity like swimming in a public theme park can be regulated in different social spaces highlights the multifaceted ways in which embodiedness is experienced within the context of sport and physical activities. There are, however, times when it is possible to swim naked, for instance, on many public beaches throughout Europe or at a designated public swimming bathhouse, such as the one in Ribersborgs Kallbadhus in Sweden. Although in this case men's and women's bodies are still separated in appropriately allocated areas, it is possible to swim in a public space without clothes and the physical experience of doing so can be considered pleasurable, indeed.

When, where and how the body is presented within a public space can, therefore, potentially cause social problems. For instance, although Angus (earlier in the chapter) described the pleasurable aspects of having an erection in a public space, this apparently innocent view does not equate with adult fears of the erection or the social fears of the 'possible' sexual body (as displayed by the management at the theme park). The heteronormative construction of the male erection, which is equated with penetration, creates a constant self-surveillance constructed in terms of how others might 'see' this shame. So, whereas the erect penis may have been mythologised throughout history as a form of potency (Miller 1995), in everyday reality and outside the expected social space for its appearance (the heteronormative bedroom), it is potentially shameful.

As mentioned above, much of the limited understanding of the physical body derives from biological explanations of heteronormative sex as well as performative constructions of gender (Butler 1993). An adult-centred formulation of sexuality sees the erotic constructs of childhood as separate from adulthood and, ultimately, a 'waiting' period prior to the onset of puberty and subsequent entrance into an adult world. Within this restricted formulation of the erotic or sexual body, as young people are not considered to be physically (biologically) able to take part in adult sexual relations, there is little room for exploring the possibilities of the body, or the potential to be found in the human condition (Pronger 2002). The reluctance to acknowledge (or lack of acknowledgement of) embodied sexuality raises questions about where this leaves the young adult or child. Are they completely devoid of sensuous feelings or awareness of sexuality? Or are they, as most adults would like to think, oblivious to it? Although a potentially controversial and uncomfortable debate, consideration of the broader definitions of embodiedness and the erotic which incorporate the sensual capacities of the physical body opens up the possibilities for looking beyond the margins.

Post-structuralist and feminist thinking has influenced the way we contemplate gender and has forced us to tackle these uncomfortable questions. Judith Butler's (1993) theorising of the discursive limits of sex and gender sheds further light on how normative gender is produced through language and how, in consequence, bodily performances create a social demonstration of normative behaviour. However, rather than being a theatrical performance or reproduction of learned existing and set social practices in the interactionist sense (Goffman 1972), these bodily performances constitute a discursive 'act' and, so, for Butler, power is formed within these acts. For Butler, performance presumes a subject is already at hand or in existence, whereas performativity contests the very notion of the subject and has the ability to create meaning. Butler starts with the Foucauldian premise that power works in part through discourse and works to produce and destabilize subjects, but goes on to contemplate performativity (particularly in speech acts but also through bodily performance) as the aspect of discourse which has the capacity to produce what it names (Butler 1993: 225). Performativity is based on an expectation of what is considered gendered behaviour. The expectation ends up producing the very phenomenon that it anticipates. Butler also notes that performativity is not a singular act, but a repetition or ritual, which achieves its effects through its naturalization in the context of a body.

Butler presents the argument that, in the case of heterosexuality, or any other dominant form of ideology, crafting or determining a sexual position always involves becoming haunted by what is excluded (1993: 34). The more rigid the position and greater reluctance to accommodate alternative forms creates a problem in that the stance needs to be defended and invariably becomes hostile to those alternatives. Thus, for her, the greater the binary distinctions which promote social understandings of male and female as separate and opposite gender positions, the greater the intolerance generated through these practices. For Butler, this can be seen in contemporary heteronormative practices and in the way institutional practices shape social understanding of the body. For instance, the social understanding of pregnancy, which is associated with a biological understanding of gender rather than within a discursive framework, produces acceptance of it being a feminine space (1993: 33). The same could be applied to sport, where the discursive framework rationalises it as an arena where male physical activity and performance is considered natural in comparison to women's sporting performance. Butler is critical of the discursive framework which positions heterosexual men in a binary opposition to women. The binary also positions homosexual men as opposite to heterosexual men and alongside women. This distinction creates a normative understanding of the heterosexual male as superior to women and gay men.

For Butler, as well as what could be considered the crux of queer theory, transformative possibilities are to be found in queer acts which provide the opportunity to oppose and destabilise normative understandings of gender behaviour. According to her, the concept of performativity is the aspect of discourse which has the capacity to produce what it names. Through repetition and continued citing, in the case of speech acts, this production occurs. Thus, performativity is, for her, 'the vehicle through which ontological effects are established' (1993 33). However, it still remains difficult to break the silences that operate within western formulations of the sexual body. For instance, the silences that occur in relation to sexuality and childhood have been analysed by DePalma and Atkinson (2006) and, according to them, reveal the discourses of the body, sexuality and gender that continue to restrict the ways in which embodied being can be contemplated and expressed. Thus, my concerns about swimming in the local pool as a 'middle-aged male' are influenced by my knowledge of contemporary formulations of what a particular body is allowed to do and how it should perform.

Thinking about how society orientates us to take 'positions' through our interpretation of what is considered appropriate highlights even more the discourses that shape our ways of being. In the case of my discomfort at swimming at the local public pool precisely because of my heightened awareness of the possibility that my 'body' might be considered unwelcome within that particular environment suggests that I might be happier if this were not the case. Sara Ahmed (2010) provides a useful analysis of the arbitrary ways in which 'happiness' is used in society. It is seen positively, often as a goal to achieve, but also as an object, something that makes one happy. Drawing on a 'phenomenology of happiness', she is able to identify how the social prescribes ways in which the individual is able to construct an understanding of what it is to 'be' happy (in the ontological sense) and, subsequently, is allowed to experience happiness.

Ahmed sees happiness as an object of desire, an 'endpoint, the telos, as being what all human beings are inclined toward' (2010: 199). In this way, happiness is important as it is a focus for future being, in as much as it suggests a future, or somewhere worth moving toward or aiming at. The notion that happiness is constructed as an 'object' and one that is desirable is significant in Ahmed's analysis as it presents possibilities.

> Happiness describes not only what we are inclined toward (to achieve happiness is to acquire our form or potential) but also what we should be inclined toward (as a principle that guides moral decisions about how to live well). Happiness provides as it were a double telos: the end of life, and the end of the good life.
>
> (Ahmed 2010: 199)

Ahmed notes the way that positive psychology has latched on to the notion that positive mental approaches help 'produce' positive orientations and outcomes. These are expressed in terms of motivational behaviours and 'looking on the bright side' However, Ahmed points out that her questions are not about whether it is possible to create happiness but rather, the interesting aspect is trying to explain and describe *the desire* for the desire for happiness.

By exploring the way in which happiness, as a speech act, has become so familiar, to explain it in a universal way is impossible. I have suggested in this book that 'fun' should be an umbrella term so that it incorporates a range of interpretations. So too can happiness be termed in this way. Indeed, it might be the case that some would see happiness as an umbrella term where fun is one interpretation of its meaning, or vice-versa. According to Ahmed,

> Happiness as a positive emotion can suggest the warmth and ease of comfort, or the sharp intensities of joy. It can be a momentary feeling, like a bolt of lightning that interrupts the night sky, only to be gone again, or the calm slow sigh of reflecting on something that has gone well. Happiness can be the beginning or end of a story, or can be what interrupts a life narrative, arriving in a moment, only to be gone again. Happiness can be all these things, and in being all of them, risks being none. If happiness does things, then does it do too much? Does happiness stop doing things by doing too much?
>
> (Ahmed 2010: 202)

In this particular case, it would be just as easy to replace 'happiness' with 'fun and enjoyment' as there are many similarities in the way that the terms are hard to define precisely. The lack of concrete meaning as well as the lack of concrete measures to assess whether happiness is being (or can be) achieved or whether an experience is fun position them in similar ways in that they are often considered meaningless in comparison with assessing a more objective form of sporting outcome, such as participation rates or physiological performance measurements (such as V02max – maximal oxygen uptake, or METs – metabolic equivalents).

Although fun, enjoyment and pleasure are inextricably linked with happiness, Ahmed describes happiness as more often seen in terms of future outcomes which are, in turn, seen as unrealistic goals. Also, according to her, happiness raises important questions about the meaning of life, in that it is hard to contemplate a life without happiness of some sort.

> Happiness is weighty not because of its point, as if it simply had a point, but because happiness evokes a point that lies elsewhere, just over the horizon, in the very mode of aspiring for something.
>
> (Ahmed 2010: 204)

Considered in this light, it might be equally salient to claim that it would be difficult to imagine what sport or physical activity would look like or be like if there were not some aspect of fun and enjoyment involved. In this way, Ahmed is making the point that contemplating the desire for the desire highlights broader ontological questions about the meaning of life and, consequently, becomes linked with questions about ethics and morality.

Ahmed's approach can be related to explorations of fun and enjoyment, particularly in the context of recreational sport and school physical education. The often taken-for-granted assumption among sport practitioners is that fun and enjoyment and their association with pleasure need to be treated with caution, or are considered irrelevant in comparison with supposedly more 'worthy' aspects such as learning skills, health education or physical activity minimum standard requirements. Ahmed incorporates an 'affirmative ethics' approach, in order to explore further the Deluzian notion of a good encounter. In doing so, she demonstrates how affirmative ethics describe the positive aspects of bodies in agreement but also, and more importantly, giving 'more to life' (2010: 214). By also drawing upon the work of Brian Massumi, she is able to contend that a good feeling, and its association with joy, delight and pleasure, is not necessarily (only) about feeling good. Consequently, Ahmed highlights that although 'words are sticky' (2010: 214) and can be used in many ways, the important point is that, whether talking about happiness or joy (or fun and pleasure),

> We cannot know in advance what different affects will do to the body before we are affected in this way or that way... being affected involves the perversity of being twisted and turned.
>
> (Ahmed 2010: 215)

Ahmed's account of the way that happiness 'affects' being provides a useful counter-argument to those for whom concepts such fun, enjoyment and pleasure are gratuitous, instances of self-satisfaction. They are far removed from this simple reading and, indeed, have more far-reaching implications and consequences upon lived experience.

Fourth dimension

While attempting to draw together the three aspects of body-reflexive pleasures, I became aware of the significance of the temporal and spatial aspects that have varying degrees of influence upon an experience. In particular, if I am making claims that there are different 'times' and 'places' that impact on the way that an activity is experienced as fun, then I need to include room for this within the circuit.

Particularly within the context of urban and leisure studies, theoretical thinking about space has been considered in terms of a 'spatial turn' or 'spatial triad' (Lefebvre 1991) and more recently by Soja (1999) through the concept of 'third space'. In these cases, the notion of space has been contemplated in attempts to extend the categories of material space and conceived space. Third space is seen as a lived space that is more than a literal space used in multiple ways, but rather a space of the friction caused by the tension and resistance between the conceived and perceived.

Consideration of a third space provides the opportunity to approach space and place as more fluid and, in doing so, to escape the often static formulations of the concept. As such, it allows incorporation of time within the space/place equation. Time has tended to be given priority within philosophical discourses, and it is an essential element of the way in which spaces and places are approached. In the context of recreational (leisure-based) sporting activities, time has constantly been constructed in terms of its relationship to work and often as 'time' away from work. Consequently, it is important to recognise how time affects our understanding of space. As Doreen Massey suggests,

> The excavation of these problematical conceptualisations of space (as static, closed, immobile, as the opposite of time) brings to light other sets of connections, to science to writing and representation, to issues of subjectivity and its conception, in all of which implicit imaginations of space have played an important role. And these entwining are in turn related to the fact that space has so often been excluded from, or inadequately conceptualised in relation to, and has thereby debilitated our conceptions of politics and the political.
>
> (Massey 2005: 18)

Massey highlights the tensions between the perceived notions of space (where there is more in our lives in terms of how we live and where we travel) and the idea that it takes less time to travel these greater distances. The problem, however, is the implication that space is considered less important precisely because technological progress has conquered distance, while, on the other hand, space has become even more of a commodity in terms of economic factors, such as land and property or social capital, such as large kitchens and holidays abroad (Tomlinson 1990, Urry 1995).

The increase in commodification of space and time in contemporary society (as seen in the Sport England market segmentation process) has an impact on the way that individuals approach sporting activities and, ultimately, are able to develop a sense of their own 'belonging' within a particular sporting space at a particular time during their lives. Massey's arguments are important as they provide further support for critical approaches to exploring sport. She provides an example of how contemporary scientific research practices have deep-seated political implications for knowledge production/construction. These highly influential research practices are managed in specific 'controlled' spaces, usually high-tech laboratories and office spaces, away from the general public. The contrast, for Massey, is that the employees move from these high-tech, globalised work environments to their homes in idyllic, rural locations where attempts are made to 'capture' nostalgic versions of family and community living. As Massey states,

> The current form of social organisation of the spaces both in the scientific laboratory and of the home are precisely attempts to regulate, though in very different ways, the range and nature of the adventures and chance encounters which are permissible. Developing a relational politics around this aspect of

these time-spaces would mean addressing the nature of their embeddedness in all those distinct, though interlocking, geometries of power.

(Massey 2005: 180)

This example can be usefully applied to the context of sporting spaces (sports laboratories, the global corporate sports industries, governing bodies) where high-tech, commercial discourses are being generated by and through elite sport at the same time as conflicting, nostalgic formulations of traditional sport are expected at grassroots level, or those spaces which could be considered as ground level.

By taking into account the temporal and spatial dimensions that influence the circuit of body-reflexive pleasure, it is worth revising the initial diagram so that it accommodates this aspect:

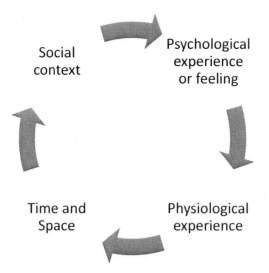

Figure 2.2 Additional dimension of circuit of body-reflexive pleasure

Acknowledgement of temporal and spatial factors within the circuit allows for a clearer understanding of how pleasure is not a 'one-off' insignificant, moment of self-gratification. Pleasure can be seen to be part of a process in terms of how an experience can *become* to be regarded as pleasurable. For example, an activity may be experienced several times before it is considered pleasurable, or maybe experienced in a space that shifts the dynamics of the circuit, such as the social and physical 'space' of a school PE lesson. In this way, the additional acknowledgement of time and space highlights how pleasure can be seen to be connected with geographical aspects of both personal experiences and social encounters. Consequently, the circuit describes pleasure in terms of a continually 'moving' process that includes elements of anticipation, experience and reflection.

Reflecting upon moments of pleasure in sport

The consideration of time as well as space in its many forms, allows us to think more about the notion of movement or process. Often, fun and enjoyment or pleasure and pain are interpreted as fixed temporal moments, a moment of pleasure or an instance of pain. However, in most cases, the assessment of whether an experience was, indeed, pleasurable or painful is made during or after the experience. So, in order to make sense of someone else's assessment, we need to understand the context of the reflection. For example, when was the reflection made? (was it immediately after the event or some time later?), what comparisons did the individual draw upon? (had this happened before?) or what were the expectations prior to the event? (did the individual anticipate pain or pleasure?)

The three descriptions of embodied experience – provided by Willy, Booth and Keith earlier in this chapter – each relate to a specific sporting activity but also demonstrate a range of physical and emotional sensations which are interwoven with the individual body as well as the social context in which the experience occurs. Physical and mental states overlap and work together and although a particular sensation, whether physical or psychological, may be the focus of the experience as it happens, the build up and subsequent reflection generate a broader understanding which can be either positive or negative.

Connell's concept of body-reflexive practices enables a broader sociological reading of embodied practice and allows the formulation of an approach to accommodate the importance of pleasure within a sporting context, via a circuit of body-reflexive pleasure. However, I have been equally drawn to the embodied, existential experiences described by Sartre (1954), of a body which could be stimulated through the senses and could, literally, 'feel' its presence in the world. To an extent, this was my introduction to 'thinking' about the body and, conversely, an awareness of my body influencing my thoughts. In addition, it helped me recognise the role of consciousness, in its many forms, and of the multiple processes which contribute to a whole experience, where factors such as anticipation and reflection are equally important. In *Being and Nothingness*, Sartre talks of pure and impure reflections. Whereas every act of consciousness makes up its own object, a reflection is consciousness of consciousness itself, but as a distortion. For Sartre, distorted reflections are based upon present expectations. Thus, for example, the reflections of an adult about childhood memories of sporting pleasure cannot be separated from the adult experiences and are perceived in a way that takes into account all previous experiences from childhood to adulthood.

In his discussion of pure reflections, Sartre troubles the concept of intentionality which was, itself, considered as a way to break away from the confines of the Cartesian cogito. So, rather than an intentional object being distinct from the act of consciousness that it is aware of (in other words it is irreflexive) in a pure reflection, the object of consciousness is reflecting or identical to the act that it is conscious of. However, without having to map out a history of phenomenology or existential philosophy, this move, or rethinking about intentionality, can be seen as a way that the concept of consciousness and reflection was developed.

For Sartre, recognition is a central factor in the construction of subject and object as identical in pure reflection. In this way, it becomes an ideal. However, if the pure reflection is an ideal, it is unlikely that we will be able to achieve it. Consequently, it is more realistic to consider distorted reflections that we can engage with purposefully. The point here is that, although the individual is aware that the reflections being made are idealised, the realisation of this is not necessarily a cause to dismiss them. Those pleasurable moments do, in fact, inform us of possibilities and guide us towards preferred ways of being. Reflection upon pleasure is therefore an important part of the process of not only being able to reflect positively upon a sporting experience, but equally to gain a positive orientation towards the activity so that one may wish to do it again.

There have been many times when I have questioned my continued participation in sporting activities, but it is the reflection upon pleasurable moments which have most resonance. To illustrate this point, I have attempted to put one of my 'pleasurable moments' into words.

Backhand down the line
I am locked in on the ball, like a hunter homing in on its prey.
My body is flowing, all my senses working in unison.
Eyes are fixed on the target, my head remains still while my limbs carry me across the ground.
I am running effortlessly, gliding as my arms move in preparation for impact.
Shoulders turn, my racquet extends behind my left shoulder, ready to swing.
Then SWOOSH – I hit the ball.
Mind, body, motion all become one as I send the ball hurtling into space in front of me.
There is a moment when I am still as I watch the ball propel forward like a meteorite crashing through the atmosphere.
Then I feel joy, I watch the trail of the ball, like a comet's tail scorching its way down the line.
I am moving again, my racquet is behind my right shoulder as if I'm about to pirouette, but my body regroups and maintains balance, ready for the next impact.

These are memories which I can relive and play over again and again. The specific details of the game (who I was playing, whether I won or lost) are irrelevant. What is important is that these stored memories are reflected upon with a sense of pleasure and are central to my desire to return to the game and repeat these 'moments'. In the same way that Willy, quoted above (from Pringle 2009), describes his pleasurable moments in rugby that make it special for him, there is a process which involves experience, not only in terms of mind and body but also including a social and historical element.

Consequently, these reflections upon pleasurable moments are both individual and social. They are memories which create an orientation to sport, enabling an individual to associate with or understand others who have had similar experiences. Reflecting upon these positive experiences provides the opportunity to make decisions about whether to continue and 'seek' more opportunities to add to this memory bank. Thus, there is an added sense of anticipation for the next time. As Sartre (1954) describes, the individual has to position him- or herself as an existential being while at the same time part of a social world where a history of social experience has been lived – and memorised. This body of knowledge informs the decisions or actions to be taken, in, as he termed, a 'progressive – regressive method', a form of looking forward by looking back.

These lived experiences contribute to and continue to create a memory bank which celebrates the joy of movement, an awareness of physicality which works in unison or rhythm with other senses. It is acknowledged that the joy of reflecting upon a backhand down the line emerges from the experience of a particular individual (subjective) moment and, although these may be considered distorted reflections, they are, nevertheless, positive and enjoyable ones that can be recalled at any time.

The important point is they need to be 'learned' in that there needs to be exposure to a range of experiences so that a comparison and a judgement can be made about what in fact constitutes a pleasurable moment. Consequently, the subjective pleasurable experience can be understood by the individual in a range of ways. The pleasure could be related to a sense of accomplishment in terms of mastery recognised through success in competing in an organised event or it could be more abstract and personalised, like my example. However, in order for it to be understood as pleasurable, the experience needs to be understood within the circuit and the contributing social, psychological and physiological factors, some of which operate with more influence than others. In this way, and understood as an experience which can be enjoyed at any level and for any range of ability, pleasure contributes significantly in the formation of an individual's orientation towards the physical body and, arguably, their further participation in sport and physical activity.

What I am attempting to say here is that my personal thoughts relating to those memories which I have determined to be pleasurable have developed over time. I have been constantly adding to my memory bank and, although the process of physically ageing has presented obstacles to the ways that I may be able to engage, access to this memory bank has assisted in decisions I have made about how I participate in sporting activities. For instance, where there have been times, after an injury or when I have developed a physical condition that might restrict how I play (for example tennis), I have been able to assess, with the help of my pleasurable memories, whether it is worthwhile continuing, albeit in an adapted form. The point is that I am making decisions about whether my continued participation will be enjoyable and, thus, worthwhile. By drawing upon a range of pleasurable memories I am able to compare and contrast different (pleasurable) experiences and assess the likelihood that I will be able to repeat any of these moments again.

Consequently, it is suggested that the act of reflection as a form of continuous 'stocktaking' of one's sporting memory bank is important. However, it may be the case that this process is not always recognised as a significant influence on an individual's participation. It may well be the case that many of those involved in sport development, coaching and physical education, do not always acknowledge the extent and significance of their own memory banks of pleasurable moments in determining their understanding of and motivation toward sport. Recognition of the 'process' related to how a sporting activity is experienced helps to take into account the 'whole package' of sport (Wellard 2002). The anticipation of and reflection upon a sporting experience (either at an individual or social level) are often equally, if not more, important than the event itself.

I have attempted in this chapter to identify some of the broader aspects of sporting participation. A sporting experience involves a range of contributing factors that occur as part of a process where elements such as anticipation, physical sensations, social aspects and personal reflection all contribute, at different times and with varying degrees of importance, to the overall enjoyment of an activity and subsequent decisions about future participation.

Note

1 Sport England is non-departmental public body accountable to Parliament through the Department for Culture, Media and Sport. Its role is to develop community sport and increase participation by working with national governing bodies of sport, and other funded partners. The Active People Survey is a large-scale study that explores participation levels in sport and recreation. It identifies how participation varies from place to place and between different groups in the population. The first survey, APS 1, was conducted in 2005. APS 7 is due to be completed at the end of 2013. Information about the Active People Surveys can be found at www.sportengland.org/research/active_people_survey.aspx. Information about the market segmentation process is at www.sportengland.org/research/market_segmentation.aspx

3 Fun and enjoyment in childhood sports and physical activity

Figure 3.1 I like swimming because…' by Pavel, aged 10
(I like swimming because it keeps you fit and jumpey. When you go in the water it feels cold but if you stay in it for long you feel hot and when I go in it I never want to go out of it and if my friend comes with me I have a race with him and when we're on the edge he pushes me off the edge and I scream ahhh.)

Pavel's description of swimming resonates with my earlier reflections of the joy that I found in swimming as a child. His drawing, along with the written description, provides a graphic account of the enjoyment and excitement that he experiences when he swims. There is a real sense of movement expressed in the drawing and the text elaborates upon his enthusiasm by telling us how he never wants to come out of the water. In Pavel's drawing we can also see how the experience for him is embodied in a range of ways that are not accounted for with a simple description that swimming, for him, is 'fun'. Pavel is able to relate to us the feeling of the water, how it affects his body when it changes from cold to hot. He is able to describe the thrill of being pushed into the water and we can understand what he means when he says that he screams 'ahhh'.

Importantly, Pavel's drawing offers us a glimpse of his world and how, through the process of creating a picture, we can share his imagining of something that he considers both meaningful and enjoyable. The drawing was created during a lesson at a school taking part in a nationally organised School Sport Week[1]. I was involved in this research project as part of a team commissioned to evaluate the experiences of the week in a sample of schools throughout England, Scotland and Wales. One aspect of the broader evaluation was a qualitative strand where a sample of schools were selected to undertake a drawing activity. In this, children who had participated in the event could draw pictures of activities during the week that they enjoyed the most. The methodological strategy was to collect the drawings during a subsequent visit to the school and use them with the children who had drawn them in order to create relaxed environments where they could talk about their own work and have at least an element of power within the research process as well as allow for their thoughts and ideas to be the centre of attention. It was considered important to present children with a non-threatening environment which was conducive to them being able to express themselves. In this particular case, it was considered that approaches which utilise additional methods, such as drawing, can encourage children to convey their thoughts accurately (Butler *et al.* 1995). According to Christensen and James (2008), methods other than direct questions help people with limited literacy or verbal skills to express their opinions. These alternative methods to traditional questionnaire and focus-group strategies can be helpful in finding the voice of the respondent rather than that of the researcher. Consequently, whereas the interview is considered a reliable technique with adults in that it allows the researcher to interact with the participant and explore and discuss their perceptions, it was considered important that children were not cued into particular responses so that results could reflect the children's perceptions. MacPhail, Kinchin and Kirk (2003) adopted similar methods where drawings were used during the interview to stimulate children's responses. Therefore, it was considered that the research approaches incorporated in this case enabled the participants' greater opportunities to express their own views and experiences within the framework of the study.

Making attempts to uncover the voices or, indeed, lifeworlds of young people taking part in an intervention designed by adults is important in that it provides an opportunity to assess how in fact these initiatives are experienced by the intended recipients. The following examples are, however, included within this chapter not only to show the importance of methodological strategies used with children but to highlight the subjective ways that the event was 'enjoyed' by the children, often in ways not necessarily intended by either the schools or event sponsors.

Adult discourses, subjective experiences

National initiatives which attempt to coordinate activities for young people are often instigated through government directives, with large-scale investments from both public and private sectors. It is no surprise that with such high stakes, there is an expectation to achieve the 'right' outcomes. It is reasonable to argue that national initiatives can provide an important and potentially positive role in the lives of young people, and it is not my intention to dispute this; rather I am more interested in exploring the competing and conflicting ways in which school-based sporting activities are experienced. It is still often the case that where interventions are developed by adults with the aim to get young people 'doing' sport, the perceived benefits for taking part obscure fuller understanding of the way that an activity may be experienced. Often, less attention is paid to why young people may want to take part and the contrasting ways they might experience it.

Sports-related interventions

There is evidence (for example, Nichols 2007, Laureus 2009, Pringle *et al.* 2011) which suggests that sports provision and related interventions can be grouped into those that divert participants away from (or deter) negative activity and behaviour and those that are designed to promote positive social development or behavioural change. Positive social outcomes in the form of crime reduction and positive community development can result from the provision of activities which divert participants from otherwise negative behaviour. This is generally achieved through the provision of activities at times and in places where concentrations of anti-social behaviour are experienced. This kind of provision also operates at the more universal level of targeting boredom generally, a rationale which underpins the delivery of many sport-focused schemes offered by local authorities during school holidays.

In the context of popular concern regarding youth-related crime and anti-social behaviour, an additional welcome outcome of a 'diversionary' activity can be the positive effect on public opinion where the perceived 'problem' of teenagers on the streets is seen as being addressed by providing young people with something to do (Laureus 2009). While diversionary activity is perceived to be more effective when participants progress to a long-term interest in it, there is limited evidence to suggest that such progression takes place in sport provision that is not part of a wider intervention (Nichols 2007). This supports the contention that a specific type of social development approach is required if long-term behaviour changes are a goal (Zarrett *et al.* 2008).

., such sport-based 'diversions' remain valuable, as there are clear ͺopportunities relating to community development and engagement which can flow from them and which may be priorities in certain contexts. Evidence shows that diversionary or deterrent-focused sport provision has the capacity to help redress disengagement and disaffection, and promote social inclusion and responsible behaviour through the capacity to engage young people that may feel excluded from society (Gibbons 2006, Sandford *et al.* 2008). Such provision can also generate a feeling of pride in community facilities and increase the likelihood that the community itself will deter minor criminality such as vandalism of facilities (Nichols 2007).

There is widespread evidence that supports the case that, in general terms, engagement in physical activity and sport has the capacity to positively benefit participants in terms of physical health improvements and through the development of positive personal and social skills and behaviours (Sandford *et al.* 2008). In the prevailing social context of concerns about the health implications of physical inactivity and increasing levels of negative social behaviour, this positive capacity indicates football-related interventions can play an important role in addressing contemporary community challenges. However, while sport has the potential for a positive impact, the achievement of positive social outcomes and behavioural changes are only likely to result from interventions that are orientated towards achieving specific social policy goals and that are underpinned by defined social processes. Examples include the development of positive social relations and attitudes through role models such as coaches or established players with community development training that are perceived by participants to be 'like me' (Crabbe *et al.* 2006, Sandford *et al.* 2008).

Getting young people to be physically active

Much of the focus for jointly coordinated and sponsored national initiatives is aimed at achieving what is considered to be in the best interests of the target group. The role of physical activity within the lives of young people is, for the most part, considered beneficial to overall development and wellbeing. Addressing wellbeing, it follows, is a reasonable vision for any government to aim for. However, as discussed in Chapter 2, the conflicting understandings of what wellbeing is and how to get it complicate the policy formation process. Often, when policy is framed in terms of an overall objective of obtaining greater wellbeing, the initial focus is not necessarily concerned with broader visions but rather single issues. For instance, much of recent government policy in England aimed at the welfare of children has been prompted more by focus on a 'children as victims' discourse, fuelled by high-profile cases of apparent failings in Children's Services to protect vulnerable children (Powell and Wellard 2008). Using the example of children's wellbeing, recent policy in England (such as, Every Child Matters 2004, The Children's Plan 2008) has consequently adopted measures which, intentionally or not, construct children as potentially at risk from a range of threats. On the one hand, this interpretation of children's wellbeing can

be viewed as a positive step toward protecting children, but, on the othe
can equally be seen to restrict opportunities for children to experience and
about the wider world on their own terms. These conflicting understandings
what is 'good' for children have had a direct impact on the ways in which children
are able to experience their bodies and explore spaces. Particularly within the
context of sport and physical activity, the messages about the positive effects are
generally described within the context of physical health and the prevention of
disease in later life (Sallis and Owen 1999). Research has also focused on the
relationship of the benefits of physical activity, sport and play to cognitive and
academic development, mental health, crime reduction and reduction of truancy
and disaffection (Bailey 2005).

Physical activity, sport and play have therefore become more interesting
recently to policy-makers and educationalists seeking explanations for childhood
behaviour and for connections between this and, in particular, cognitive development (considered a key aspect of wellbeing). Indeed, wellbeing and health
have been defined as important 'products' of children's physical activity, sport
and play, thus providing the basis for their inclusion in educational curricula and
out-of-school programmes and provision (Bailey *et al.* 2009). This focus on the
role of physical activity, sport and play has emerged from a general belief that
the health and wellbeing of children should be a national concern, in a way which
presents young people as being 'at risk' of not doing enough physical activity.
Consequently, in the quest to address the perceived imbalances within social
wellbeing, there has been much focus on children's bodies and minds, particularly in relation to physical and educational development. UNICEF, for example,
attempted to incorporate a measure of external 'reality' and subjective responses
to identify a league table or 'dimensions of child wellbeing in rich countries'
(UNICEF 2007).

There has been much recent debate about children's wellbeing expressed in
terms of 'health' and potential risk of obesity (Gard and Wright 2005). Although
well intentioned, the potential problem is that continued focus on specific
outcomes has assigned many other equally important aspects of a young person's
development to the sidelines, ultimately impeding the quest for overall wellbeing
that is proposed as the main objective. Consequently, as suggested in Chapter
2, there appears to be a continued lack of understanding about the interplay and
connectedness between physical, social and psychological ways that individuals
develop an orientation toward a physical activity and, indeed, their own embodied
identity.

The influence of government policy initiatives has played an increasing role in
the way that schools have developed mechanisms to respond to national directives. Evans *et al.* (2007) demonstrate how a performative culture (Ball 2004) has
influenced the ways that schools operate and ultimately interpret and disseminate
'knowledge'. They suggest that

> Such changes have been underpinned by a powerful culture of individualism
> which has celebrated the notion that everyone, irrespective of background,

to succeed and 'get on' in work, sport, leisure and health
of excellence, self-improvement, individual initiative and
ty, at the expense of acknowledging how these processes
nd constrained by the social and material conditions of

(Evans *et al.* 2007:55)

In particular, there has been an increasing status of the role of health within school understanding of the rationale for PE and sport. To the point where, regarding the PE curriculum (NCPE),

> Most teachers would now rationalise it's (the NCPE) provision and emphasis in the curriculum with reference to their capacity to help resolve health concerns, invoking unproblematically the equation more sport = more health.
>
> (Evans *et al.* 2007: 57)

The requirements of performativity have ultimately caused the complex discourses of health to be reduced to a focus upon weight, diet and exercise. These concerns are driven by what Evans *et al.* describe as 'new health imperatives' which 'prescribe the lifestyle choices that many young people should make, particularly in relation to physical activity and diet.' (2007: 57). Consequently, there are tensions between the rhetoric of individual expression and a much more limited performative agenda with the reality being that young people are more likely restricted by the requirements of schools that are unable, or find it difficult, to resist the directives of broader social policy.

However, although the argument for developing a national approach to delivering sport and physical activity to young people is based upon all schools receiving similar provision, it is not always the case that what happens at ground level is necessarily the same in every school. For instance, Green *et al.* (2007) in their examination of participation in sports in secondary schools in England and Wales found that the involvement of 15–16 year olds in different sports and physical activities varied substantially according to the school they attended (2007: 76). They suggest that, 'neither changes in NCPE since 1992 nor the broadening of PE curricula by teachers have resulted in the displacement of competitive sports or "traditional" team games' (2007: 83). At the same time, however, there is evidence of newer sports and individual games being incorporated, but any change, according to Green *et al.*, needs to be read alongside the evidence of continuity.

Dudley *et al.* (2011) in their review of Physical Education and School Sport interventions suggest that 'PE teachers, researchers, and education and health policy-makers need more evidence on how the diverse nature of PESS practice and pedagogy can play a central role in positively influencing young people's physical activity participation, movement skill proficiency and enjoyment of physical activity' (2011: 374). It is with this in mind that we have set out to

explore in more detail the diverse ways that young people experience a s|
based intervention.

Wellbeing and health

Although attempts to generalise about wellbeing and health (both individually and collectively) are constrained by subjective interpretations, when sport is brought into the discussion, more often than not, it is incorporated as a positive view, where sport is a life-enhancing activity that contributes to wellbeing and physical health (Bailey 2005, Sallis and Owen 1999), educational attainment (Bailey *et al.* 2009) as well as reducing youth disaffection (Sandford *et al.* 2008). Much of this focus is generated through broader rhetoric and, to an extent, deeply entrenched views among sports professionals and politicians alike of the health benefits of sport.

As I mentioned in Chapter 2, some aspects of sport, such as extreme sports and combat sports, which might contribute to individual wellbeing, have become increasingly popular (Wheaton 2004) although from a health perspective may be considered dangerous in terms of risk of injury and harm (to individual participant and in the case of, for example, mixed martial arts, the opponent). Similarly, at elite level, in the quest for achievement and success, continued high-profile cases of athletes found using performance-enhancing drugs (for example, Ben Johnson, Marion Jones and Lance Armstrong) have also highlighted the external pressures faced by professional sport players, but also how conflicting messages are being presented in relation to the mostly undisputed claim that elite performers are role models and inspirations for children and young people.

There is also a further debate about the role of the state. In some instances, what the state considers to be good for individuals because it enhances their health, may be perceived by such individuals to detract from their personal wellbeing. The smoking ban would be one such example. However, the debate is wider than the needs of the individual in contrast to the imposition of values from a paternal-istic state, because the concept of public health, the public good and the wellbeing of society should also be considered. From this viewpoint, initiatives such as the smoking ban, while detracting from the wellbeing of individual smokers, can be seen as enhancing the health of society as a whole by enhancing wider wellbeing by allowing non-smokers to enjoy smoke-free environments and by reducing societal incidences of heart disease and lung cancer associated with smoking. There is often a tendency to develop this argument further in economic terms, such as the cost to the NHS of treating such diseases, or the loss of productivity in the workplace, but the negative impact on the wellbeing of friends, family and colleagues of smokers who develop health problems is also an equally significant issue.

Given the above, it is evident that there is still room for more discussion on wellbeing, health and sport, particularly when considered in terms of adult discourses which have a direct impact on the lives (and wellbeing) of children and young people who may not necessarily have a voice within these discussions and

...ses. It is often the case that, in relation to the role of sport, ...ns between those who cannot see compulsory provision ...n a force for good; those who are critical of sport, largely ...y see as the evangelising of many who are unequivocal about ...nefits; and those who agree that sport may not be good for all, ...an be good for some.

Con... ..., I am not intending to provide conclusive answers about the role of sport in young people's lives, but rather I attempt to highlight the arbitrariness of the *processes* through which young people are able to participate in sporting activities within the school environment and, in particular, the contrasting ways in which these activities are subjectively experienced. As Kirk (2010) suggests, the idea of PE is up for grabs and, as evidence suggests, if school sport and physical education (PESS) remain a defining influence in young people's early experiences of sport and their embodied identity, how it is 'delivered' is crucial in shaping an individual's orientation to future adult participation in sport and physical activity.

School children's experiences of a sports-based initiative

Within the context of the National School Sport Week (NSSW), and throughout the evaluation, the overwhelming response from students during the analysis of the larger survey was that they enjoyed the activities and relished the opportunity to try new sports. Table 3.1 below provides an overview of the responses generated in the quantitative survey which, in turn, provides a rationale for selecting the key themes which I concentrate on in this chapter. The majority of the questions were developed to provide an indication of how the core aims of the week were being received.

Although these responses did not (or were not originally intended to) elaborate upon the ways in which the children experienced or, indeed, 'enjoyed' the activities, it is, however, through analysis of the qualitative accounts gathered during the school visits and, in particular talking with the younger children about their experiences using their own drawings, that I was able to compile a much richer 'picture' of the ways in which the event was experienced. What became clear was that the children offered a broad range of explanations for their positive experience of the sports week. The following quotes, for example, provided an early indication of the varied ways in which the children were engaging in the event and how it had meaning for them:

> *I enjoyed playing new sports. It was so special because it was fun.*
> (Primary pupil, Scotland visits)

> *One of the values, equality, so even if you're disabled doesn't mean you're not equal to everyone else.*
> (Secondary pupil, Wales visits)

Table 3.1   Secondary pupils' ratings for different aspects of NSSWs (n=1,853)

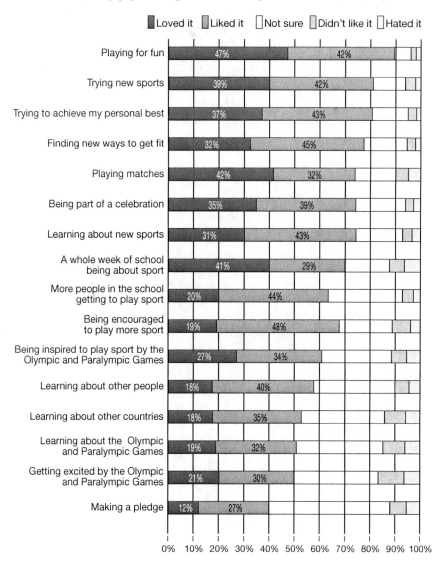

It's made me want to do sports more. I used to think sports were boring.

(Primary pupil, England visits)

It is really enjoyable no matter how good/bad anyone was, everyone could join in.

(Secondary pupil, England, online survey)

It was good to work as a team with the infants.

(Primary pupil, England visits)

The primary school children in particular expressed their enthusiasm for taking part in activities outside and with friends. The two drawings below (Figures 3.2 and 3.3) provide examples of how the children were able to convey representations of activity and enjoyment. In these cases, there were clear themes which emerged relating to the pleasure experienced in physical movement as well as being outside, enjoying the physical environment.

Figure 3.2 Me skipping outside

Figure 3.3 Running race in the field

However, and more importantly, if we are attempting to 'read' these drawings and gain an insight into the impact of the activities upon the lives of young people, we need to get a sense of what went on before and after these pictures were drawn. Although the drawings are informative if read alone, they do tend to prompt further questions about the context in which the activity was experienced. In order to provide further explanation of the key themes which emerged during this research I have focused on three specific examples. These relate to: *opportunities, subjective experiences* and *embodied pleasures.*

Opportunities

Figure 3.4 depicts two girls 'having fun in tennis'. Without the accompanying caption, one might view the picture as being of one girl, as the figures are strikingly similar, indeed, almost a mirror image. This indicates the drawing abilities, but may also hint at the way in which children 'see' themselves and other

Figure 3.4 Alice and Carrie playing tennis

children as being either similar or different. It is not clear who drew the picture. One may presume it was Carrie, as her face is clearer and she is slightly more the centre of attention. However, at face value, the picture represents themes of activity and enjoyment. The girls' bodies are poised in preparation to make contact with the tennis ball. Their readiness for this may indicate that they have knowledge of the technical aspects of tennis and may have played many times before. There is also a sense of playing in unison, a suggestion of rhythm in the way that they are hitting the ball to each other. Consequently, there is a representation of movement.

These are my interpretations of the picture and may be representative of an adult reading of the image – what I think the child who has drawn it has been thinking and wanting to convey. It was, in fact, Alice, who had drawn the picture and in subsequent conversations about her drawing, she was able to provide more detailed information about her own story behind the picture. She explained how she had drawn 'a girl' playing tennis and had only included her name and her friend (Carrie) afterwards. When asked further questions about her experiences of playing tennis during the school sport week, she provided a narrative which added greater dimension to the drawing. Indeed, a context which would not necessarily have been understood if the images were taken at face value.

I discovered that Alice and Carrie had never played tennis before. Their school had been able to pay for a tennis coach to come in during the school sport week and provide sessions for the children. The school did not have its own tennis courts, so had to make do by marking out temporary lines on the playground and using portable nets. Subsequently, Alice's picture may now also be read as a representation of how the children had been taught 'how to play', in that the children are clearly presenting preparation techniques.

Alice told me how she had seen tennis on television before and, although she had thought she would like to 'have a go', there were no courts at the school or in nearby parks or, indeed, any local tennis clubs. She explained how she had enjoyed the physical experience of 'hitting the ball' and that she had felt 'excited' when the racquet had connected with the ball and went where she wanted it to go. Having fun was therefore a combination of an embodied experience of a sport along with the opportunity to do this *with* her friend Carrie. They could both enjoy their experiences together and be able to share the memories of the experiences with one another. Consequently, the interpretation of fun that Alice revealed is that of a complex intersection of the physical, psychological and social.

When Alice was asked if she would be able to continue playing tennis, she told me that it was unlikely as there 'was nowhere to play' and they did not do tennis in physical education lessons. This was confirmed by the headteacher during a subsequent interview with him. I asked Alice if she thought she would be able to play again when she moved to secondary school next year. But, again, she said she was not certain whether they played tennis there at all. Consequently, it could be suggested that for Alice and Carrie, the fun and enjoyment (and potential for them to continue playing a sport into their adult lives) that they had experienced during the school sport week was merely a tantalising glimpse rather than a concrete foundation.

Subjective experiences

Whereas Alice's 'story' related to her personal experience of taking part in a specific sport, the children's drawings were not always necessarily about themselves. For instance, Tommy was more interested in portraying what he *saw* and his drawing (Figure 3.5) may even be considered as a representation of his own world view, or *lebenswelt* in the Weberian sense; for what is revealed in the picture is a glimpse of what Tommy considers important, in as much that he wants to include it in his depiction of what he remembered about the event.

Consequently, the narrative is not about him winning or competing in a sport against others, but an observation of the activities his school friends and other non-sport-related memories that he considered relevant. Thus, we are shown, in addition to the activities, representations of social interaction, movement and nature. Tommy was fascinated by the worms and worm-mounds on the playing field. When I spoke to him about the picture, he told me how he had enjoyed this particular day when there were a series of sporting activities held on the school field. He liked being able to go outside the classroom and in this case watch all the activities. Although he was able to take part in several of the events, such as the relay race, he said that he enjoyed more the atmosphere of the 'whole' event and being able to cheer on his friends. I asked him about why he had included the worms in his drawing and he explained that he was interested in the way they lived under the ground and had wondered what they must have felt with all the running above them.

Figure 3.5 Tommy's sport festival

Tommy's teacher told me later how he was really interested in nature and science and that he had appeared to enjoy the school sport week because of the range of activities on offer and the way that it was 'different' for him in relation to PE, which she said that he was not particularly keen on.

Embodied pleasures

In this study –similar to others that explore children's engagement in physical activity – the ways in which children and young people experience sport is often reported through general descriptions such as 'fun' and 'enjoyment' without further explanation. However, as described above, the subjective interpretations of what constitutes a pleasurable experience is more complex and these draw upon a range of social, physiological and psychological factors. For many children, the experiences of a sport or physical activity are an embodied process through which they learn about their own limits and capacities.

So, where the picture below (Figure 3.6) could be read as a light-hearted depiction of some of the cruel aspects of a contact sport such as dodgeball, the boy who drew it was able to explain to me why he found playing the game exciting.

For, Luke, the 'fun' experienced in taking part was a combination of things, in particular, for him, a 'fear of being hit' by the ball. His drawing, he explained, was an attempt to depict the 'agony' of being hit and, at the same time, show how he had observed the different ways in which the body reacted in different situations. For him, there were different levels of pain – sometimes it hurt, other times it did not – but this sense of not knowing, if the ball did hit him it, what it would 'feel like', added to the sense of excitement and anticipation. Similarly, Luke explained how the knowledge of how it felt when the ball hit him contributed to feeling a thrill when he was throwing the ball at another person. Consequently, not only was Luke grappling with intrinsic pleasure but also complex issues relating to achievement, forms of power, existential understanding of the physical body, as well as sadistic and masochistic embodied pleasures. Indeed, the popularity of an apparently innocuous activity such as dodgeball may be more readily attributed precisely to the power relationships enacted between the thrower and the dodger. However, for Luke, the joy is in the literal embodied thrill of throwing, running and dodging. Although he is unable to articulate with sophistication the complexities of such an activity, he is able to demonstrate an awareness of why a particular activity is considered more than just 'fun'.

What did become clear, however, was that the pleasurable aspects of taking part were significant for a range of competing and complex reasons, and these, importantly, played a central part in the children's experiences and recollections. Consequently, the embodied experiences described reveal a much more sophisticated reading of pleasure than the generally held view that it is an intrinsic, individual and, ultimately, hedonistic expression (McNamee 2005). The pleasures that the children describe incorporate elements of the social, ontological, physiological and psychological that I described in Chapter 2. These experiences

Figure 3.6 Luke playing dodgeball

contribute to a stockpile of pleasurable memories which can promote positive orientation toward specific activities, which act indirectly (as opposed to a direct outcome) to promote healthier lifestyles.

Enjoyment as an additional outcome or goal?

The examples presented above were taken from research conducted during the National School Sport Weeks held in 2010, 2011 and 2012. A major theme throughout this initiative was the Olympic and Paralympic Games, held in London in 2012. From the time that London was announced as the host for the Games, many nationally funded sporting initiatives became increasingly influenced by them in some form of other[2].

The global appeal of the Olympics also attracted sponsorship from large private organisations, keen to share the attention that such an event attracted. The NSSW was no exception and was supported by a private sponsor working in collaboration with a government-funded agency who administered the programme. The Olympic theme was considered by both parties as being an integral aspect of the sports week, and guidance was offered to schools who registered to take part about how to incorporate an 'Olympic' feel during the week by adopting Olympic values, such as personal best and fair play.

During 2010, the evaluation noted that school children were not particularly aware of the Olympics at that stage. Indeed, in that year, many schools, although continuing with broadly based Olympic values, had focused more upon the 2010 football World Cup in South Africa, as the belief was that their students would be able to relate to something more current. However, the NSSW was successful particularly in the way it was able to provide new opportunities, especially for children to try new sports or engage in activities that had not been available before.

In the 2011 National School Sport Week, the emphasis on London 2012 became more influential. The teachers felt that the Games were more relevant to the children as the event was nearer and there was also growing coverage in the media. Many schools used the Olympic and Paralympic Games as a vehicle to introduce sports that were not usually covered in their physical education curricula. A separate week-long event enabled schools to organise external sports groups and coaches to provide taster sessions for the children or for the PE staff to run activities themselves, such as these trips to a newly opened local aqua-centre (Figures 3.7 and 3.8).

By the time of the 2012 Sport Week, the Games were only weeks away and schools had been exposed to a heavily publicised national torch relay, which had travelled an extensive path across the UK. Consequently, many schools were able to incorporate additional activities in order to simulate a festival event of their own. These included holding opening and closing ceremonies, running torch relays and having award presentations. This 'festival' approach was enjoyed by the children and was reflected in the responses in a larger survey as indicated in Table 3.1 earlier in this chapter. Here, the fun element was important as well as

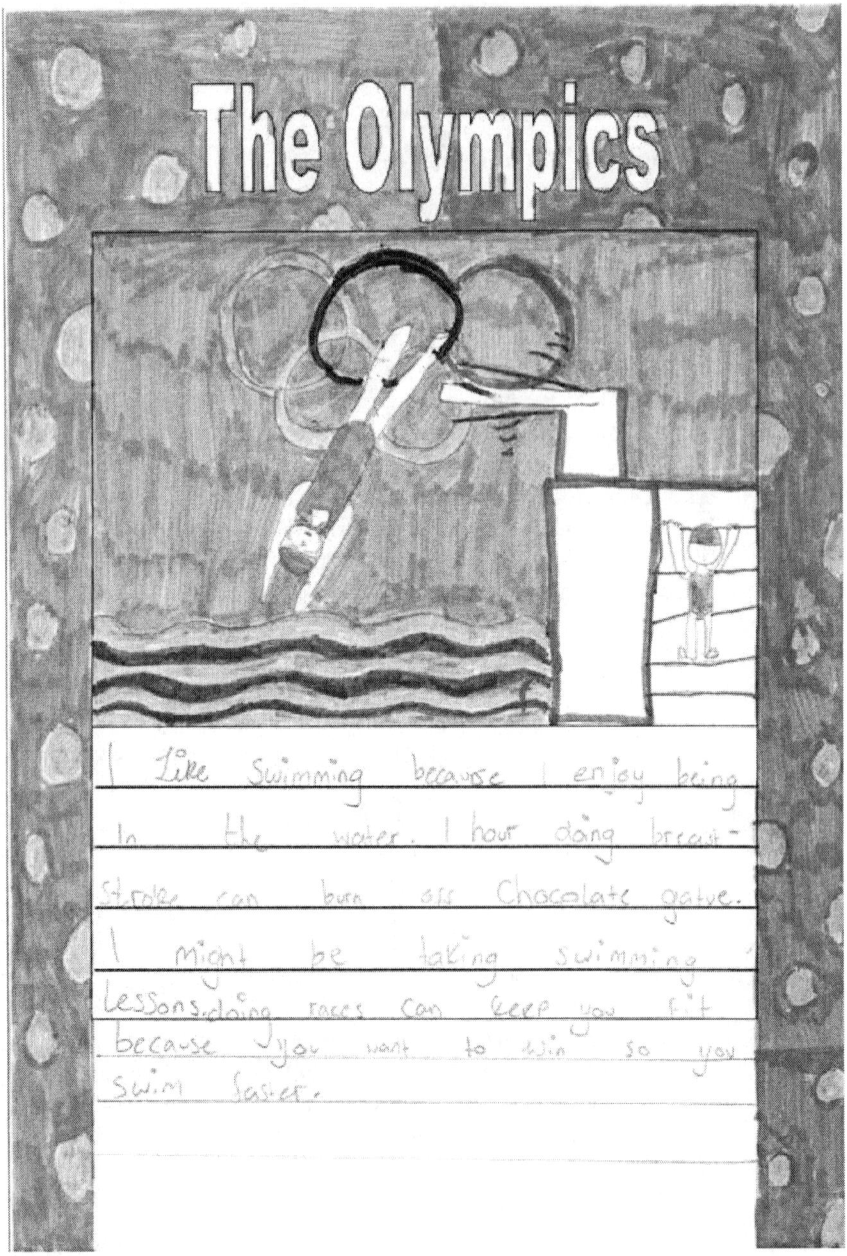
The Olympics
I Like Swimming because I enjoy being
In the water. I hour doing breast-
Stroke can burn off Chocolate gatue.
I might be taking swimming
Lessons. doing races can keep you fit
because you want to win so you
swim faster.

Figure 3.7 Why I like swimming (1)

Figure 3.8 Why I like swimming (2)

having opportunities to try new sports. For the older students, being able to make choices about the activities they took part in was also an important factor in their evaluation that the sport week was fun. However, an equally important aspect for all the children was that many of the activities, because they were new, could be approached without being encumbered by pre-expectations of ability, or lack of it. The influence of both teachers' expectations and personal perception of ability is seen as a constant factor in the way that children determine whether sport and PE is for them (Evans *et al.* 2004, Wright and Burrows 2006, Wellard 2006b). Being 'good at' sport, or not, is repeatedly offered as the reason a sport may be considered enjoyable or not.

So, many schools were able to offer Olympic-themed sports and, in particular, were keen to provide opportunities for their students to try Paralympic sports. In many cases, during the larger quantitative survey, children reported that they enjoyed trying out disabled sports. An example can be seen in one school visited during the 2012 NSSW where, as part of their sport week, they had an 'Olympic and Paralympic day' during which a range of activities including goalball (a team sport designed for blind athletes) were offered. This activity was extremely popular, as the drawings and descriptions in Figure 3.9 indicate.

The children's descriptions highlight an embodied enjoyment of the activity where taking part entails more than just an ability to develop sport-related skills and offers a broader appreciation of physical attributes that are often taken for granted. Consequently, the children reported their enjoyment in being able to incorporate other sensory skills, such as hearing (2) and spatial orientation (4), that did not rely on sight alone. In particular, the activity of goalball, where blindfolds were worn to restrict sight, neutralised existing abilities and enabled the children to enter the sport on a level playing field. This allowed a range of embodied experiences for the children, not necessarily purely sport related and regardless of their sporting ability. Goalball was enjoyed in this way because it was an example of a disability sport that the children could literally empathise with. However, as indicated in (3), other activities were enjoyed because they were noticeably different.

The research highlighted that although a national intervention, such as the National School Sport Week, was a considerable success and was received enthusiastically by the children who took part, the ways in which the children experienced the event did not necessarily reflect the original (adult) aims. While many of the children may have enjoyed their experiences and may ultimately choose to continue to play sports, the relevance of the adult messages relating to healthy lifestyles were less clear. What is also important, however, is that national initiatives such as this one provide new opportunities and alternative contexts away from the usual routine of the school day. They compare with other 'events' that occur during school time, such as an annual school trip to a museum; often, for the children, the purpose of the trip is forgotten. What is more significant is the event itself as an experience and the sociable aspects of it, such as, for instance, the coach journey, the café, the gift shop, being with and seeing other people. All of this can be seen to contribute to a 'festival effect' (Weed *et al.* 2010) where

Figure 3.9 Experiences of goalball

the cumulative effects of a larger-scale social event outweigh the actual focus. Indeed, much of the appeal of leisure-based sport and physical activity for adults is experienced in the social aspects (Svoboda 1994). This theme is explored further in Chapters 4 and 5.

Whereas, in the context of school-based sports, physical education finds itself in the position of having to fulfil its performative obligations (Evans *et al.* 2007) as well as being required to identify and nurture the next generation of elite performers (Bailey and Morley 2003), these alternative events are important in that they can provide experiences of physical activities from a different perspective and, possibly, a foundation for later adult leisure pursuits. However, this is not to overlook the importance of recognising the different forms of 'resistance' that teachers present to external demands. As Tinning (2010) suggests, it is not necessarily the case that all PE teachers will harbour health agendas in the prescribed form, or are fixated on elite performance. Indeed, within the context of the National School Sport Week it was not always the case that the coordinator would necessarily be a PE teacher. In many primary schools, the first point of contact was a headteacher with no specific PE background. Thus, resistance to external directives could be seen not only 'within' PE, but also among teachers in general, with differing perceptions of the role of PE and school sport as well as of the external directives.

The intention throughout this chapter has been to generate questions about the role and idea of PE, in the way that Kirk (2010) has suggested. There are many questions that have arisen relating to the way that PE is provided, taught and perceived not only by PE practitioners themselves, but by a range of other 'interested' parties. Consequently, I have deliberately concentrated on trying to keep the experiences of the children and young people, who are the ultimate beneficiaries of such schemes, as the central focus. Questions that emerge can then be discussed in relation to the future of PE and, indeed, the future of external funded initiatives, and of national healthcare provision.

Notes

1   The National School Sport Week is a national initiative in the UK administered through the Youth Sport Trust with sponsorship from the Bank of Scotland and Lloyds TSB. The programme started initially in England and Wales in 2008 and was introduced in Scotland in 2010. These annual events were designed to motivate pupils to do more sport by celebrating and profiling PE achievements in schools, and providing a platform from which to launch new sport-based initiatives. A central focus for the sports weeks has been themes based upon Olympic and Paralympic values. The Centre for Sport, Physical Education and Activity Research (SPEAR) at Canterbury Christ Church University was commissioned to evaluate the programme by the Youth Sport Trust in 2010, 2011 and 2012.

2   In 2008, the Labour Government (in power at that time) outlined a policy strategy with three main headline goals. These were: (1) Inspiring young

people through sport: Offer all 5-to-16-year-olds in England five hours of high-quality sport a week and all 16-to-19-year-olds three hours a week by 2012; (2) Getting people more active: Help at least two million more people in England be more active by 2012; (3) Elite Achievement: Aim for fourth in the Olympic medal table and at least second in the Paralympic medal table in 2012 (Department for Culture, Media and Sport (2008), 'Before during and after: Making the most of the London 2012 Games', London: DCMS).

4 Sport, fun and enjoyment for the 'non-sporty'

That's why I like this club, because it's not serious, it's not a curriculum activity, it's not something that you have to do. It's something that you do, you do if you want to do it and you can say yes or no. It's a very relaxed atmosphere where you get to see those friendships and mix with all abilities. So we help to include, you know, people.

(Jodie aged 19, participant in community boccia club)

The focus of Chapter 3 was children's experiences of a week-long school sports event. The event was held in school and was aimed at all levels of ability. The advent of the Olympic and Paralympic Games in London 2012 was a major influence, with both government and national sports organisations wanting to utilise the popularity of the Games to provide a sporting legacy of additional participation. Although the evidence suggests that the Games were extremely popular as a national event, it is still not clear whether they will inspire more young people to take up sport. As Weed *et al.* (2009) found in their review of previous Olympic Games, evidence suggested that it was more likely that those people already participating in sport on a regular basis (in other words, sports enthusiasts) would be inspired to take up a new sport. Indeed, it appeared to be more the case that an individual without any predisposition for sport would see the pursuits of Olympic athletes as being even further away from their own reality.

This chapter explores further the notion of the 'non-sporty' and the ways in which sport may be considered enjoyable for those for whom sport in its traditional forms has not always been appreciated in the way that it has for a sports enthusiast. Physical activity, sport and play more generally have therefore received renewed interest recently from policy-makers and educationalists seeking explanations for childhood and adolescent behaviour and for connections between this and, in particular, cognitive development (Bailey *et al.* 2009). Consequently, wellbeing and positive health benefits have been defined as important 'products' and outcomes of children and young people's engagement in physical activity, sport and play. This has provided the basis for their enhanced inclusion in educational curricula and out-of-school programmes and provision throughout the

United Kingdom. The renewed focus on the role of physical activity, sport and play has emerged from a general belief that the health and wellbeing of children and young people should be a national concern. Therefore, in the quest to address the perceived imbalances within social wellbeing, there has been much focus on children and young people's bodies and minds, particularly in relation to physical and educational development. As mentioned in Chapter 3, UNICEF attempted to use a measure of external 'reality' and subjective responses to identify a league table or 'dimensions of child well-being in rich countries' (UNICEF 2007).

In particular, much of the recent debate about children and young people's wellbeing has been expressed in terms of 'health' and the potential risk of obesity. Although well intentioned, it could be argued that continued focus on specific outcomes has assigned many other equally important aspects of a young person's development to the sidelines and has ultimately impeded the quest for overall wellbeing proposed as the main objective. Arguably, failure to acknowledge the broader subjectivities of a young person' lifeworld can be related to a continued lack of understanding with respect to the interplay and connectedness of the physical, social and psychological.

It is also relevant to note at this juncture that much of the attention focused on the wellbeing of children and young people is generally framed within a discourse of family or education, where the child is essentially considered as being in a developmental stage prior to adulthood. In contrast, the focus for the adult is usually framed within a discourse of 'work' and the relationship to an economic system in which the individual's principal role is to contribute to the labour market. Although policy can be seen to acknowledge issues relating to inclusion and exclusion, invariably it is shaped through an economic focus and relationship to the work environment (Jeanes 2010). Consequently, the position of children and young people is located outside the 'normal' understanding of the tax-paying worker.

Leisure activities for children and young people are, therefore, constructed within a context where their participation is not accounted for in the way of an adult worker, where there is a clearer distinction between work and leisure. In this work/leisure equation there is (arguably) a heightened element of choice, although the interpretation of leisure participation still remains complex (Stebbins 2006). For the child or young person, however, it could be claimed that there is less 'freedom' to choose to take part in recreational leisure activities than for a wage-earning adult. For children and young people, opportunities to take part in leisure are understood either in terms of informal play or those situations which are provided by adults. In the case of school provision, the manifestation of any form of leisure opportunity is expressed through an instrumentalist version whereby the outcome becomes the focus. For example, reducing obesity by increasing exercise levels, or providing additional sport as a stimulus for academic achievement may become the basis for the planning of activity engagement for school-aged children and young people.

From the brief discussion above, it is already clear that there are many factors which complicate the analysis of physical leisure activities aimed at children and young people. So, the focus in this chapter is to explore the subjective experiences of children and young people by drawing upon the examples of those taking part in a nationally directed initiative in order to: first, identify whether the specific ways in which children and young people can enjoy sport and physical activities are considered in the same way, and, second, explore the relevance of embodiment as a factor within the participant's positive engagement, particularly in the way that the broader aspects of taking part in sport influence enjoyment and continued participation.

Before discussing any of these issues further, it is important to attempt to gain a perspective within the context of the young people I am writing about. I have suggested previously that research which aims to present the experiences of young people should make attempts to 'listen effectively to children's voices' (Wellard 2007: 11) in ways that capture the subjective context. I draw upon examples taken from two different national sport initiatives. The first explores the experiences of one group of young people taking part in a nationally funded scheme to encourage sporting activity. Looking specifically at their perspective helps to consider the complex subjectivities at large, and at the same time, allows focus to be maintained on the chief recipients of the intervention. The second example draws upon research conducted with young people taking part in a nationwide initiative where sporting activities were provided within local communities as a form of 'doorstep' sport.

Fun and enjoyment in a community boccia club.

In this first example, the focus is a boccia club which was established for young people with special educational needs and physical disabilities. The club was developed through funding provided by a national initiative, the Change 4 Life (C4L) School Sports Club programme, sponsored by the UK government and administered by the Youth Sport Trust[1]. In this particular scheme, funding was provided to local schools wishing to establish one of seven sports clubs targeted at 'less active' children and young people as an 'after-school' club[2]. The seven sports offered were table tennis, badminton, volleyball, fencing, handball, wheelchair basketball and boccia.

It is worth noting that I am not attempting to make generalisations about the plight of disabled young people per se, but rather use this opportunity to explore the subjectivities found in a nationally driven, sport-based leisure activity (provided for young people) which can be 'read' in a number of ways. Also, I am not suggesting that the experiences of those involved in this sports club are necessarily alternative or 'other', but theirs can be interpreted alongside many other voices that contribute to the formulation of contemporary youth experience. In this particular case, the justification for focusing on the boccia club is that, although issues relating to the body and physical ability are more obviously foregrounded, the club was formed within the broader context of it operating as one of seven sports clubs offered through a programme aimed the 'non-sporty'.

In this particular example, I concentrate on the experiences of two participants, Jodie and Nick, and by giving them central stage, the intention is to understand the issues which they felt were important in their lives and to assess these in relation to broader debates about the benefits of participating in sport-based leisure activities. At the time of the research, Nick was 18 and in a 'gap year' before going to university, while Jodie was 19 and one of the older participants of the group (who ranged from 15 to 19).

The boccia session was initiated through consultations with the local Partnership Development Manager (PDM), the School Sports Coordinator (SSCo), Val, and representatives from disability groups at local Further Education (FE) colleges. The original intention was for it to be held at the Special Education Needs (SEN) school where Val taught, but it was considered that the club would work best if it was in a central, community-based location, with facilities appropriate for all potential participants. Val's background in SEN had influenced the approach to the boccia session, but the specific focus of the club in terms of the type of provision and the target groups meant that it was distinct from a general school PE context.

The boccia session was, consequently, held in a modern, recently built, community facility near the city centre. The facility was provided by the community charity Centre, established by the local authority. There were other activities being provided in other rooms at the time which contributed to an enhanced community feel (in contrast to a school multi-use games area or a village hall). The participants were recruited mainly from local Further Education colleges within the area and through disability group networks. There was one participant who lived further afield, but regularly made a 60-mile round trip in order to attend, as there was nothing similar in his local area.

The idea for starting a Change 4 Life club had been developed through Val's SSCo role in collaboration with the area PDM as well as her work with local young people with disabilities. Val felt that the community needed a particular type of provision; 'one which could accommodate a range of younger people with SEN', and in particular, older teenagers. The sessions had started in November 2010, mainly through the enthusiasm of the coordinator. It was advertised in local colleges and through the PDM/SSCo networks. They had been well attended with an average of between 14 and 16 participants throughout. The participants at the sessions observed presented a range of physical disabilities and SEN. Several were in wheelchairs with extreme physical disabilities and many others had severe forms of Autism and Asperger's syndrome. Val also supervised two volunteers who led the activities. One (Nick) was 18 and on his gap year before going to university (to study either medicine or sports science), the other (Chloe) was 15 and still at school (Year 11) and had a background of mild learning difficulties. Chloe had been offered the volunteer role in order to boost her confidence (which, according to Val, had 'helped enormously'). The participants paid £2 for the one-and-a-half-hour session, and this covered the cost of the venue and refreshments. The club sessions, although not operating within the context of a school, were clearly providing opportunities for young people with SEN and physical disabilities to take part in an enjoyable physical activity. They were also offering opportunities for the volunteers, who were gaining from the initiative in different ways relating to their specific disabilities and in their broader personal and social wellbeing. In addition, by holding the club in a community centre, the club was considered more accessible to addressing the needs of a wider local disabled community. The parents and carers who brought and collected their children were extremely supportive.

Although the atmosphere was very relaxed and informal, the sessions were well structured so that the activities were varied. In one session observed, there were about four different activities based around a boccia theme and they included both team and individual elements; the participants were clearly enjoying taking part. They were also extremely supportive of each other. For example, there were many occasions when one of the participants, because of their disability, would take longer during their turn, but this did not appear to bother the rest of the group who waited patiently and expressed support.

The majority of participants had been attending regularly since the club began. During my first visit, I was able to speak with one participant (Jodie) during a session break. She had cerebral palsy and was restricted to a wheelchair. Jodie had been active in helping Val establish the session and when asked what she liked about the club she referred to the social and informal atmosphere saying that she loved being with the others and doing boccia in a relaxed manner. I arranged that on the next visit I would speak in more depth with Jodie and Nick, and their experiences of the club follow here.

Jodie's experiences

Jodie explained how she had been involved and how the boccia club started.

> *I wanted to start up a boccia club up because it was something to do and my support worker said that it would be good for Val to have someone who is disabled to help her, and one of the main reasons is there is not much for disabled people to do in the area and for them to mix with other disabled people. I went to, I think I told you this before, to a sheltered accommodation place and then I moved out of there because there was no funding and they used to do activities there like boccia and other things. I had played before... but I'd always been scared to play boccia before. It was important where I lived, it was a big thing – everybody played boccia and there were competitions.*

Jodie explained how there had been boccia provision in the past and that it had been assumed that she would like to play competitive sport by those involved in running the residential homes that she had lived in. For Jodie, however, the main motivation in taking part in boccia had been that it provided the opportunity for social experiences. The specific sport itself was less important than the chance to be with friends. She explained further in the context of what would happen if the boccia session ended.

> *It's not so much the boccia; people would lose the friendships,. the place to meet. I mean I'm quite ok, I get to go out, but I should imagine some people would lose the chance to go out. Because other times it's difficult to go out with the carers and stuff.*

Although Jodie was herself severely disabled, she was still able to contextualise her personal situation with others for whom she felt were in greater need of care and benefited even more from taking part in the boccia club. It was important for Jodie to get the message across about her and other young people's reliance upon community services. It became apparent that Jodie felt equally restricted in terms of her ability to take part in taken-for-granted community leisure activities. The social elements of meeting friends and 'mixing' with other people were considered an essential part of her and the other participants' wellbeing. At the same time, Jodie had learned to present the 'value' of such a club to an outsider by drawing upon the broader range of possible benefits that taking part in a sporting activity could develop. However, the fact that Jodie was aware of the need to 'sell' the club to us did not detract from the impact the club was having on a group of young people with a range of physical and mental disabilities and their opportunities to engage in social leisure activities. For instance, Jodie was able to describe how the club was valuable for others as well as herself.

> *It is also some people's main outing, something they can look forward to, and offer plenty of different opportunities in the future. Yeah, I mean there's Lucy and she has severe autism and suffers quite a lot with it and she's quite a reserved person and seems to have come out of her shell and seems to have enjoyed it tonight. I think she has started to feel comfortable and knows that we all have disabilities.*

What was important for Jodie and the other participants was that the club was considered their own time, which is often an aspect of young people's lives that is overlooked in provision of leisure activities and in play provision for younger children. The additional factor that many of the participants in the boccia club were restricted by their physical capabilities meant that opportunities to be independent (in a very broad interpretation of the term) were limited. Jodie was able to explain further the importance of the club in terms of personal time and space.

> *So it also provides continuity as well for us and we can also be away from the carers for a couple of hours and be able to be independent with your friends.*

Significantly, what Jodie is emphasising is the importance of a community leisure club, such as this one, as a mechanism for some form of semblance of self-autonomy, which needs to be interpreted within a broader context of leisure provision for adults who invariably have greater agency in their leisure choices.

I asked Jodie what she felt was for her the most pleasurable aspect of taking part in the club; she responded:

> *The best thing that I like about the boccia is… it's a very relaxed atmosphere and you get to socialise and cheer each other on which you wouldn't do in any other sort of boccia club and it's relaxed. And it also opens doors for other opportunities. For example, I'm now looking at doing a leadership in boccia course. So the opportunities are there, but they are not forced upon you. And I kind of just like the relaxed atmosphere.*

Jodie's experiences in the club had changed her attitude toward boccia, in that she realised that there were opportunities to do more activities which were not necessarily related to playing competitions. She had realised that by becoming more involved she could help others who wanted similar things from the club. In particular, she felt that the sport itself was starting to develop.

> *I feel the boccia has come on and developed and people have developed – they've got to know each other and socialise and cheer each other on. So people's confidence develops.*

However, although boccia had been incorporated in the programme because it was a Paralympic event, Jodie felt that it was not necessarily a certainty that the games would help all disabled groups.

> *I think a lot of the big groups, big set up groups will be helped, but to be honest with you, I think we need the groups like this so that more people get to know and then they get to progress. And more smaller communities get to know about disabled people. To be honest with you, there's not much for disabled people around. I think the more people get to know about boccia, the more they'll tell other people and the more they'll get to know about disabled people and that's how I feel a community develops. It starts small and it grows.*

Nick's experiences

Although Nick could be considered 'able bodied' in comparison with Jodie, he did not have a conventional background in sport and physical activity. Nick had not been interested in sporting activities in the past and also offered a conflicting account of his engagement with sport.

> *I'm not a typical person who plays sport. I really didn't like sport, I never took part. I was always the kid in PE lessons who would have the note, who wouldn't do PE. I never saw the value of sport. It didn't appeal to me. I was never really athletic. I could do it but I was never really motivated by it.*

Nick explained how he had been more interested in other leisure activities and only 'discovered' sport at the later stages of secondary school.

> *I'd go out with friends, but there was never really anything to do with sport. I used to play an instrument when I was younger, but it wasn't until about Year 10 when I was about 15 in core PE lessons we did the Level 1 award in sports leadership. And that changed everything for me about sport. It was a different pathway in sport and seen from a different perspective it enabled me to see the value of sport and really set me on a different track. It was just... I was never ever going to be an Olympian, no way, but... I wanted to achieve something in sport. I think I always wanted to achieve but had never been able to. I was always able to speak in public and things like that – so I had some of the natural leadership qualities already which meant I was quite successful doing the (leadership) award and things. And I had quite a good School Sports Coordinator in my school who got me to do a load of things in coaching and I got involved that way. One of the courses I did was the TOP/ Youth Sport Trust award and that was led by Val who runs this club and I really got into it then. So, I then moved to sixth form and the school I moved to had a boccia club. So I got involved in that when I started sixth form. It's kind of all gone from there really.*

Nick had been introduced to the broader aspects of involvement with sport through educational and leadership roles in the senior years of his school days and this pathway created opportunities that he had not been aware of previously. Boccia was one such activity.

> *I hadn't come across boccia before we did the leadership course. We all did that with the aim of doing a festival of some sort. And after that I thought I'm not really going to do anything with it. It wasn't my main sport – athletics and netball that's what I tended to do and what I coached more of. But there's something different about boccia. I think it's more the group you work with rather than the sport itself that appealed to me – and I think that's how I got involved.*

Nick explained how the club had developed to where it was at the present time.

> *Well this club is independent of the club that I started in at the school. The one at the school was already established when I got there. I was a sixth-form student then. I'm on my gap year now before I go to university. So I'm still helping out there. I now really enjoy it actually. In maybe the other sessions you'll consider yourself as the coach. But, I don't know, I don't really consider myself as the coach for this, it's more of a facilitator really. You have the potential to stand back; like... I coach a lot of other sports now. I coach Year 2 multi-skills up to regional squads in netball, under 18 level, so I coach quite a broad spectrum of abilities and backgrounds and things. I*

don't know, this is just kind of abstract to that and I think I just get something out of this that I don't get out of the other things I do.

In a similar manner to Jodie, Nick's experiences of sport were not gained through a traditional pathway. His interest had developed at a later stage through engagement with wider aspects of involvement in sport, in this case as a leader, or, in his words, a 'facilitator'. The boccia club was, therefore, more than just a specific sporting activity; the social aspects were much more important for all of those who took part. Nick was able to equate his own perceptions of sport with those of the participants.

I think it is the focus of the group that is centred round the social aspect. I don't think it could be centred around anything else and I think what make things like this work so well is the fact that they are socialising with others. I'd seen some C4L stuff before and I'm doing some stuff with other school kids where they send a group of Year 6 kids up to us and we do a variety of sports and talk about healthy activities and things. But that is more of the educational thing, a form of raising awareness, whereas this is just, I think it is about making a provision. Those other kids could quite easily get involved in sport if they chose to, whereas these guys (in the boccia club) don't have that ability. So in comparison to all the other things I have done, this is very different but definitely in a good way.

In particular, and central to the programme's original aims, there was a clear sense that the club had developed into being more than just a 'boccia club'.

It's not just about boccia. Boccia is there, it's the sporting activity and they do it, but it's not what they come for at all. I think if you asked any of them, I don't think they'd say, 'I come along to develop my boccia skills, to enter competitions.' They come for the social aspect, to make friends and keep up with people and I think it's a break for them that they don't often get. Some of the carers have that experience, so you can have a joke... When I first started out in disability sport it was hard to know how far you could push... not push, but see how far you can go. I mean some people can take a joke, others can't. It's like any situation, with disability some might react differently. So you have to be careful and tread the water to see what it's like. But now, I know when to joke, what to say and when they lose their temper, which they do from time to time, I know how to calm them down and what to say.

On a personal level, although Nick was able to benefit from taking part in terms of adding qualifications and volunteering experience to his CV, he was keen to point out that this was not the primary motivation.

Oh, it's not that at all. If that is all you get from volunteering – something you get on your CV – then I wouldn't do it. It's so much more than that. I coach at a lot of other different groups and this is the one that I enjoy the most. I really look forward to it. The other sessions, you get paid and things like that. But this is what I enjoy doing; I enjoy doing things like this. You learn so much. Not just skills, but communication skills. Things like empathy, what it is to be different and how things are not always black and white. And I think in schools, I don't think you'll learn as much as you could about things like this and it's just a really good experience to have. I really enjoy this.

The ways that Jodie and Nick were able to experience the boccia club as worthwhile, relevant and enjoyable were developed through a range of social factors, shaped by an embodied formulation of sporting identities. In this particular case, experiences in the activity cannot be fully explained only through participation in the boccia session, but have to take into account the way that engagement is influenced by a range of social, psychological and physiological factors, some of which have more significance at different times. These subjective responses shape not only participation but also initial orientation and subsequent reflection. Consequently, it is important to take into consideration the ways in which individuals create understandings of their own bodies and in turn develop understandings of their own social and physical identities as well as others.

The potential for pleasurable experiences through physical leisure activities has to be managed within social understandings of a range of discourses, such as gender, sexuality, age and ability, which may ultimately prevent or diminish one's ability or willingness to take part. As I described in Chapter 2, the concept of body-reflexive pleasures helps us understand how social and cultural factors interact with individual experiences of the body. This in turn creates a need to recognise not only the social forms and practices which underpin the individual's ability to take part in sport, or any other physical activity, but also the unique physical experiences of bodily based expression. Indeed, it is within this context that it is equally important to recognise the range of factors which contribute to the experience of pleasure (or not). Thus, if we apply the concept to an individual's experience of a sport, it can be seen that consideration needs to be made of the social, physiological and psychological processes which may occur at any level and with varied influence. Pleasure is therefore central as part of a circuit of interconnected factors which determine the individual experience. For example, Jodie's overall enjoyment of the boccia session was not necessarily gained from a physical thrill, often associated with participation in sport, or a sense of achievement gained through 'winning', but rather pleasure generated through the social aspects of engaging with other young people. As suggested in the previous chapter, this is an aspect of sports participation often cited by young people as well as adults within an amateur/leisure context but still overlooked by many sports providers and policy-makers.

Also central to Jodie's embodied understanding of the boccia club was her own perception of disability and the broader social construction of it. Although disability is now widely accepted as a 'socially created' condition which is a product of an inherently 'ableist' society which attaches ideals and standards of acceptability to an 'able' body, there remains a failure to accommodate the differing needs of people with impairments (Kumari Campbell 2008). Within this 'social model' of disability, exclusion and disadvantage are viewed as the products of socially created barriers, which may be political, attitudinal, environmental or economic, and can be effective alone or in combination (Shakespeare 2006, Barton 2004).

The introduction of a 'Big Society' approach to addressing community needs (or failings) has been championed by the current Conservative Government in the UK (Stott 2011). The assumption here is that local communities will be best able to look after their own interests through collaboration with private sector and voluntary provision. However, as Runswick-Cole and Goodley point out, particularly in the case of the disabled, the Big Society 'represents an unwelcome regressive move back to models of disability based on charity and pity and away from affirmative and rights-based models' (Runswick-Cole and Goodley 2011: 884).

For the participants at the boccia club, physical disability issues were only part of the equation. Although there were obvious disadvantages relating to each participant's specific physical condition, economic factors played an equally significant part in their lives, in a similar way that affects many other disadvantaged young people, disabled or not. However, as Cara Aitchison suggests, in relation to leisure provision for disabled people, dominant discourses of exclusion have invariably equated social exclusion with economic policy (Aitchison 2003: 966). Indeed, although it was clear that Jodie enjoyed taking part in the boccia club and was able to describe it as being important in her life, external funding issues had always been present and there was a constant threat that the boccia club would not be able to continue. Jodie not only recognised that funding had a major impact on her own personal circumstances but that it was a significant aspect within the lives of many other disadvantaged people.

> *There was an education centre where they did courses and stuff like that, but most of the funding ran out and I had to move and I lost all my community. So, I became very angry if you like as I didn't have any friends or things that were familiar, so I wanted to be part of something that was familiar, something that I could gain some more friends from, something that wasn't too serious, something where all abilities could mix.*

For both Jodie and Nick, knowledge that the boccia session was included within the C4L programme because of its relationship to the Olympic and Paralympic Games in 2012 was less relevant to their motivations for wanting to take part in the club. The theoretical rhetoric is that the potential seen in the Paralympics reflects broader research into sport and physical activity which suggests that sport is a social institution which not only 'mirrors' society by reflecting prevalent norms and relations, but can also provide a site in which to transform them (DePauw 1997). In this case, the general view is that sport provides the means to challenge negative stereotypes through the presentation of disabled people as very 'able' when supported by empowering and enabling environments, thereby challenging negative stereotypes (Arbour *et al.* 2007). It may also support attitudinal change and social integration by increasing exposure to 'difference' in a positive context (Winance 2007). Statements and assertions made about the Paralympics transfer this capacity for the promotion of attitudinal change and social inclusion to the Games' attributing such positive qualities including the promotion of equal value in the joint organisation with the Olympics and the challenge to negative stereotypes in the projection of positive role models and ability (Landry 1995). Equally, much is made of raised disability awareness that results generally from heightened media attention and specifically through changes in the discourses of service provision and town planning which have to happen to fulfil the practical requirements of hosting the Games (Gold and Gold 2007).

However, there is little research on the impact of the Paralympics, and what is available suggests that the Paralympics are either marginalised or ignored and have assumptions made about them that are neither quantified nor evidentially based (London East Research Institute 2007). Even if the case for the Paralympics can be successfully presented, it does not necessarily mean that the benefits will extend beyond those disabled athletes who took part. As Weed (2010) argues, in relation to the Olympic Games, there is little evidence to suggest that they can motivate those other than the already sporty to participate further.

So, while the recent focus in the UK on the Olympic and Paralympic Games because of London 2012 is helpful in placing some of the above issues in a wider public debate, it could be argued that it still leaves many important questions about people (able and disabled) engaging in everyday sports and leisure activities that are never intended to be serious (in the elite sport sense) but are still, however, significant and meaningful to the participant. In both cases (the Olympics and Paralympics), where the focus is on serious (able or disabled) athletes, there is the risk that those (like Jodie and Nick) who want to pursue sport-based leisure activities in a less competitive fashion will feel further marginalised.

Even in publicly funded national initiatives aimed at getting young people more active, there is still confusion about what wellbeing actually means and often claims are made in the 'interests' of others. As suggested in Chapter 2, these are more often than not uncritical adult visions of what physical activity for young people 'should look like'. Presumptions about what is 'good' for young people have a direct impact on the ways in which young people (and adults) are able to experience their bodies and explore leisure spaces. The experiences of the participants at the boccia club highlight that the conflicting interpretations of the 'non-sporty' are better explained through an approach which recognises a broader 'embodied' formulation.

In particular, Jodie and Nick's articulation of the importance of wider 'social' aspects of leisure activities suggests that this is an area which needs to be considered carefully, especially if the intention is to gain an understanding of individual wellbeing and happiness. What is significant is the relevance of wider subjective social and pleasurable benefits which are generally overlooked but are equally important in the lives of those who participate for a variety of reasons, although they are not necessarily easy to 'measure'.

Fun and sport on the 'doorstep'

At this point, it would be useful to provide another example of a community-based project – StreetGames[3] – where I was involved in research exploring the experiences of the young people taking part. The example provides support to the claims about the arbitrary ways in which the participants experience and, ultimately, enjoy the activities offered.

The evidence for this evaluation came through two methods of data collection. First, a survey of participants using 'A Young Person's Feedback Card'[4] which was designed to assess the 'direction of travel' of young people's sport engagement in terms of regularity of participation and attitude to sport. Second, a series of visits were made to sites where the local project was being delivered.

Like the Change 4Life School Sports Club programme that Jodie and Nick were taking part in, StreetGames had as its core aim to get more young people taking part in sport and physical activities. This particular programme's focus, however, was more specifically aimed at providing 'doorstep' activities to children and young people in the hope that by providing opportunities to play sport in spaces close to home it would motivate them to play more.

In a similar way to the boccia club described above, many young people who attended regularly were encouraged to help out with the activities. There were several examples of participants who had found these opportunities rewarding. For instance, Hakim was a StreetGames volunteer who began by taking part in community-based sport sessions when he was younger. These were organised through a local professional football club. When these activities stopped there was a period in which nothing was provided in his immediate area and it was at this point Hakim approached the community sports coordinators, which led to StreetGames sessions starting. At this stage, he started some coaching and asked if he could volunteer and then trained further. He explained how he had wanted to volunteer because *'I didn't have this when I was this age, I had to play with the older kids and didn't want to.'* Consequently, a multi-use games area in the centre of his local estate was redeveloped through funding provided by the local council. Hakim was invaluable for the scheme, as he knew the estate well and most of the children who took part, many of which he had known since they were born. He explained how he now had ambitions to develop football pathways for other children because there were many with parents who had only limited financial resources. The lack of financial resources was a significant factor in excluding many of the children from taking part, although Hakim felt that there was a lot of talent and enthusiasm to be found on the estate.

Hakim's story was similar to many other narratives provided by the participants during this research. Although Hakim's story provided a really positive aspect of the impact of the programme, it also revealed an underlying 'problem' with many such sport-based initiatives. In this case, football was undoubtedly the main activity on offer and enjoyed by those who took part in these sessions. However, there was an expectation that everyone would like football, to the extent that there was complacency about the 'universality' of football as the game of choice for all boys. Conversely, the alternative expectation for girls was dance. Although many coordinators commented that they had consulted with the young people about what they wanted to do, it appeared the case that a majority of the boys taking part came to the sessions either with a liking for football already or having had no notable experiences of other sports. Consequently, although football was popular, there appeared to be missed opportunities to engage boys and girls who did not necessarily like football, or who would have liked to play but had not had previous opportunities to develop the required (or expected) skills. In contrast, the research found that where there was provision of non-traditional sports it appeared to engage young people that were less inclined towards sports participation and the traditional school offerings.

The broader aim of the research evaluation was to explore the impact of the programme upon young people's engagement with sport. However, during the study, it became apparent that the young people were enjoying the experience of taking part for a variety of reasons, and not always specifically related to the sporting activity. For the younger children, it was sometimes intimidating having older children there, but this concern was alleviated by the presence of adults and the older volunteers. Many children mentioned that they felt safe in the StreetGames sessions, more so than if they were to arrange an informal play activity of their own in a public space. For instance, one girl explained:

> *At first we were scared and shy as there were older girls there and we didn't know how to dance... now it's like a team.*
>
> (Female participant, aged 11)

In addition, some of the children liked the sessions being structured for them as it provided the opportunity to develop skills. In the case of a StreetDance session offered at one of the sites, it was heavily structured, but the girls liked this as they felt it provided them an opportunity to progress. Similarly, many of the boys taking part in football at several sites commented on the positive aspect of having organised games arranged by the coordinators (albeit in a relaxed manner), in particular, where provision could be made for someone to take on an officiating (referee) role.

> *I enjoy having something competitive and organised.*
>
> (Male participant, aged 18)

> *I like it when we get to play different age groups; gives you the opportunity to learn new skills.*
>
> (Male participant, aged 15)

For many young people, the sessions were providing their only chance to take part in organised sports sessions outside school or college. In some cases, there was little opportunity in college at all. However, not all of the sessions offered a full range of opportunities to engage all young people. For example, one session was held in a youth centre with a small sports hall and an additional room with sofas to relax in. It was popular with the local young people as a place to come to away from the streets and especially so during the cold winter evenings. Several young people told me that they would like to take part in sports activities in the hall, but these were invariably dominated by the boys who wanted to play football all the time. This sentiment was expressed by boys and girls alike, for instance:

> *I sometimes play sport, but the same boys play football all the time and I'd like to play tennis or badminton.*
>
> (Male participant, aged 18)

The coordinators were often aware that they needed to provide a broader range of activities, but many felt restricted by what they could offer. This was also echoed in sites where football dominated. Many of the coordinators felt that it would be difficult to provide alternatives as the participation rates were high in the football sessions and the participants were enjoying them. At one site, the coordinator was attempting to introduce new sports and encourage more girls. They had worked with a local 'Active Women' scheme, and tried to introduce alternative sessions such as Indian head massage and arts and crafts activities with the intention that they may be able to move the girls on to sport. But this did not work as, according to the coordinator, the girls attending had found it difficult to concentrate and the whole point of the programme was to avoid the sessions being too school-like. By that stage, most of the girls just wanted to chat with their friends and 'watch the boys'. The coordinator felt that in this particular case, it would be better to have got the girls interested in sport at a younger age.

Nevertheless, the StreetGames sessions could be seen to contribute significantly to broader local community efforts. Often this was related to the fact that the sessions allowed young people to take part in enjoyable activities where there was often no realistic alternative.

> *If I wasn't doing this then I would probably be playing Call of Duty.*
>
> (Male participant, aged 15)

> *Probably be bored out of my mind at home or on the streets, causing no good if I am honest.*
>
> (Male participant, aged 17)

> *I really like being able to play, if the session wasn't on, would 'just stay inside'.*
>
> (Male participant, aged 10)

If I wasn't here I would probably be bored on a Friday.

(Male participant, aged 14)

Just hang about; when club is not on bad stuff kicks off. It's a bad area.

(Male participant, aged 16)

Overall, there was a clear message from the young people taking part that the sessions provided opportunities which they enjoyed and which they recognised as a valuable alternative to playing computer games, being bored, staying in, or hanging around the streets with a potential to get into trouble. There were many other stories to be found among those taking part in the clubs we visited during the research in both the Change 4 Life School Sports Clubs and StreetGames programmes. They provide further examples of the different ways that sporting and leisure activities can be experienced as positive and enjoyable. At the heart of this debate is the need to acknowledge that, within the context of recreational sport, and in similar ways to the experiences of the schoolchildren in Chapter 3, enjoyment is experienced in a range of complex ways which may impact on wellbeing in ways not always predicted in large-scale initiatives.

Notes

1 The Change 4 Life School Sports Club programme was introduced in England in September 2010 and an evaluation of the programme was conducted by SPEAR throughout the first year. A range of quantitative and qualitative strategies were incorporated in the evaluation. However, the focus in this chapter is one of the qualitative case studies, a boccia club provided for young people in a large town in the north of England. In this particular case study, three separate visits were made to the club between the months of January and June 2011. Observations were made and interviews conducted with session leaders and participants. A semi-structured format was adopted in all the interviews in this case study as well as others conducted in the broader evaluation research. This format led to an open-ended discussion and invited the participants to base their responses on their own experiences, focusing on what they considered to be relevant or important. At the same time, having a structure in terms of a series of prescribed questions aided analysis of the transcribed material and allowed identification of themes from the responses.

2 'Less active' children and young people are defined by Youth Sport Trust as those doing less than one hour of physical activity per day.

3 StreetGames is a national sports charity in the UK that aims to deliver sporting activities to the doorstep of young people living in disadvantaged communities.

4 The survey cards were designed to strike a balance between simplicity and quick completion, and the need to gather data on participation, attitudes and

engagement from a significant sample of young people. 510 feedback cards were returned and analysed. Site visits were made to six regions between December 2010 and February 2011. In each case, I visited the site with another colleague. An interview was conducted with the lead coordinator and a series of informal conversations were held with the young people taking part.

5 Embodied fun and enjoyment in adult recreational sport

I've been running [fell] for nearly 30 years. People ask why. I have only one answer. There's nothing on this earth I enjoy as much than getting onto the hills and feeling the wind in my lungs, and heaving my body up the slopes. The smell of the rivers, the feel of the wet grass slipping under my feet, the sounds of the birds as I scurry through the brush. The feeling of wholeness and peace, even in the middle of the gruelling run, is almost indescribable... It took a long time to get there, and to have a mindset where I can be alive there. And I am alive, because you never know what you will face on the run. Out there is unpredictable and untamed.

(Charlie, 35, quoted in Atkinson 2010: 124)

In the previous two chapters, the focus was on the different ways that children and young people enjoy and experience sporting activities. In the transition to 'adult' sport, it could be claimed that the significance of fun as a factor in sporting experience becomes further marginalised with the additional emphasis upon more serious aspects, such as competition, skill performance and achievement. However, as Charlie describes above, there is much more to be gained from recreational sporting activities. Indeed, Charlie's description of his embodied enjoyment of *being* out in the hills highlights the existential elements of engaging with physical activity in ways often neglected when attempting to understand a sporting experience. Central to Charlie's experiences of (among other things) pleasure, pain, peace and engagement with the environment was the recognition that it had taken a long time to develop an understanding of the multiple layers of pleasure that he could experience. As I suggested in Chapter 2, recognition that a sporting activity is not necessarily an instant occurrence is important. In most cases, developing a positive orientation toward an activity requires a process of discovery where assessments are made at the time and afterwards, and where a memory bank of pleasurable moments can be developed.

The intention in this chapter is to continue to explore the theme of embodied fun and enjoyment in sport participation but focus upon qualitative, empirical research conducted with those considered 'outside' the usual lens for sports research. In this case, not professional elite sports men and women or young male (serious) sports participants, but rather the middle-aged 'amateur' sports enthusiast. I have chosen qualitative interviews (sporting-life histories) with two middle-aged people who take part in sporting activities for enjoyment. It is often the case that many participants in sport remain 'invisible' from scrutiny, however by focusing upon the embodied experiences and pleasures found within the context of sport and physical activity 'life-histories', broader interpretations of what participation entails can be assessed. These particular methodological approaches have been utilised successfully in previous research where the intention was to gather material which provided qualitative accounts of experiencing the body in sporting contexts (Wellard 2007, 2009). The material in this chapter has been taken from a series of semi-structured interviews that were conducted at differing sites for physical activity and sport between 2009 and 2012. Like most leisure-based sports and physical activities, participation is primarily a voluntary decision and, consequently, the physical, social and emotional experiences need to be considered in this light. At the same time, by taking into account the previous historical experiences of sport and physical activity, there is the possibility to provide a narrative of the respondent's experiences of sport while recounting a meaningful story.

Adult recreational sport and physical activity

In Chapter 2 I discussed the contrasting ways in which pleasure can be experienced within the context of sport. For example, one of Pringle's (2009) interviewees, Willy, described his 'moments' of pleasure that marked out rugby as an activity that he wanted to return to again and again. I also mentioned Booth's (2009) description of the physical aspects of surfing and the pleasure he found in the physiological release of endorphins within his body that taking part produced in terms of an embodied 'rush'. Both examples provide informative accounts of adult sports and, in particular, highlight the significance of embodied pleasure during the sporting experience. However, while these accounts are relevant, it is important to recognise that the majority of these experiences are described within the context of traditional, heteronormative, (younger) adult, male sports. However, the third example included, provided by Keith (Wellard 2009) of his own personal memories of sport, not only highlights the relevance of embodied reflexive pleasures but also reveals ways that allow us to extend the gaze beyond the traditional focus of sport studies.

Each of the three descriptions of embodied experience relates to a specific sporting activity but also demonstrates a range of physical and emotional sensations which are interwoven with the individual body as well as the social context in which the experience occurs. The contexts of age, gender and sexuality can be seen in terms of how they inform the ways in which the activities are experienced, or, indeed, allowed to be experienced. However, regardless of the ways in which the individual gets to the point of taking part, the three accounts are similar in that the participants found something pleasurable during the activity and the memory was such that it warranted a desire to return. Thus we could argue that in many cases in the context of traditional sport, the social construction of age might act as a barrier to participation more than the physical effect of an ageing body.

More recently, there has been increased focus upon the experiences of the older adult within the context of sport and physical activity (Humberstone 2010, Dionigi *et al.* 2011) and within a growing field of literature related to a 'sociology of ageing' (for example, Featherstone and Hepworth 1991, Woodward 1991, Twigg 2004). These insights are welcome, although in many cases, within the context of a *sociology* of health *and* ageing, the definition of aged is more in tune with the final stages of life and the care requirements of the (ailing) very old. This remains in stark contrast to the youth-based focus of sport research, particularly at elite level, where peak levels in many sports are considered to decline after the age of 25 (Berthelot *et al.* 2011).

Studies of sport and the middle-aged and older adult demonstrate the difficulties of the categorisation of 'the old', but they also draw attention to many invisible participants in recreational sport as well as the significance that sporting activities have upon these people's lives. For instance, Phoenix and Orr (2012) conducted research with older sports enthusiasts in order to gain qualitative understanding of the meaning of these activities within their lives. The following extract is from one of their interviewees, a 60-year-old cyclist.

> *Once kitted up the sensation of anticipation sets in. The bike ticks as I wheel it down to the road; I sense how light it is and how pleased I am to own such an aesthetically pleasing bike. My cycling shoes (impossible to walk in) crunch on the gravel path of my house. I switch on the GPS, step astride the bike and clip my shoes in to the pedals, select a gear and ride. There is an immediate sense of freedom as well as anticipation.*
>
> *Then there's the weather. Riding in rain, hail, snow, blazing sun, fog, strong wind or a combination of all has 'pleasures'. Ideally the temperature should be in the 20s, no wind or precipitation, but we don't live in California so overcoming weather conditions becomes one of the challenges that separates rides. I have come home soaked to the skin or frozen so cold that it's hours before I'm warm again, and yet I cannot imagine life without those extremes, it would be so 'beige'. Being always safe and comfortable would drive me mad. All of us need a bit of discomfort induced by our own behaviour and our own fault! That way we know when we are having a 'nice' time.*
>
> (Rod, 60, cyclist, quoted in Phoenix and Orr 2012)

Rod's descriptions of his experiences while cycling provide evidence of the embodied enjoyment that he gains from taking part in this activity. These experiences draw upon more than 'just' the physical act of cycling, but rather involve an array of emotional, sensory and social factors that ultimately contribute to the formation of his embodied being. However, as is the case with any brief insight such as in these two extracts, there are many unanswered questions and the reader may remain wanting to know more about his background and experience of sport.

Has he always cycled? Has sport always been important in his life? Has he taken part in other sports?

In order to explore in more detail the influences, motivations and orientations toward sporting participation, I have incorporated examples of two middle-aged sports enthusiasts, Gary (49) and Elizabeth (45). They have been selected, not for their sporting prowess or success in their chosen activities, but because, like Rod and Charlie (above), the sport in which they take part is considered, for them, important enough to have become a regular aspect of their lives. The inference is made that, through their continued participation, it can be assumed that they are 'freely' choosing to take part and, because of this, it is fair to say that there must be a degree of enjoyment experienced. With this in mind, I felt that it was important to provide detailed accounts of their 'stories' so that the reader could make assessments about the subjectivities found in the experiences as well as note any similarities to personal experiences. Their stories have also been included as they do not sit comfortably within any of the 19 market segments constructed by Sport England, described in Chapter 2. Consequently, it is often the case that such stories and experiences fall off the 'radar' in terms of recognition, either as legitimate sports participants in their own right or as potential recipients of local or national funding initiatives to encourage sport participation. Nevertheless, their stories provide valuable insights into the ways in which individuals approach sporting activity and how compartmentalising specific 'types' of participant limits possibilities for engagement.

Gary

In my study *Sport, Masculinities and the Body* (2009), I incorporated a series of interviews with men who took part in sport at a recreational (amateur) level. These men had experienced sport during their childhood in contrasting ways. Some had extremely positive experiences, others had not. However, in their adult lives, they all reported to me that sporting activity was a major aspect of their lives. In that particular study, I had purposefully concentrated upon the overarching research theme, which was related to the performances of hegemonic masculinity within the context of sport and the centrality of the body during this process. However, a key theme throughout this research was the importance of enjoyment in taking part. I noted the following in the conclusions to that book. Much of the research highlighted how sport and physical activity was considered enjoyable and this aspect may provide a useful entry point into further investigations. Although the research was primarily located within a sociological evaluation of masculinities and body practices, the sport setting provided the opportunity to consider developments within contemporary sport. I described how the men who took part in the study had varying abilities and differing experiences of sport, but in almost every case there was a common sense of enjoyment from the physical experience of taking part in a sporting activity. Much of the sense of pleasure was experienced in early childhood in various forms (Wellard 2009: 141).

Those early experiences of sport and physical activity were gained in a variety of settings. Many of the men had not enjoyed school sports and PE but were, nevertheless, able to recollect experiences that had remained with them, and these ultimately provided incentives to continue as adults. In one example, I explored the experiences of Simon and Gary to highlight how 'successful' participation in sport is shaped by social constructions of what is considered to be the 'appropriate' bodily performance for taking part (Wellard 2009). In this particular case, the social expectation for hegemonic forms of masculine performance prevailed and, consequently, the ways in which Simon and Gary were able to negotiate participation contrasted dramatically. Simon was able to perform in the 'expected' ways and was, consequently, able to reflect upon an untroubled history of successful sporting participation. Gary's case provided a contrast in that, although he was the same age and had grown up in the same town, his experiences of, in particular, school sport were marked by his distinct inability to perform hegemonic masculinity. His reflections were informative in relation to my arguments about the dominance of specific forms of masculine performance that still operate within the context of sport. However, I was struck by the determination that Gary (and many of the other marginalised men within the sample) displayed in wanting to continue to take part in sport or physical activity in some form or other.

That particular interview was conducted in 2000 and it was by chance in 2010 that I heard how Gary had taken up swimming in recent years, to the extent that he was participating on a daily basis. As I was exploring the themes of fun and enjoyment and had been considering my personal experiences of swimming, I thought it would be interesting to see if I could talk to him again. And, I was able to conduct another interview with Gary, this time ten years on.

At the start of our conversation, I reminded Gary of the previous interview and the themes we discussed. I told him that I was interested to find out more about how he had made a decision to take up swimming and why it had become a big part of his life now. He began by explaining how he had first decided to start swimming.

> *I went on holiday a few years ago and I went to Greece with T and we took some photographs and stuff like that and I went swimming with him at the beach. T is a good swimmer and I was ok at doing the breast-stroke and we had a nice holiday, but when we got the photos back, I looked at the photos of myself and I thought, 'My god, I've got to do something.' That's when I started taking up swimming and T said to me, 'Shall we go to the pool?' and I said, 'Yes, let's go,' and we went for the first time and I've been literally every day since. So basically, to start with, I did it to lose weight.*

Gary's appearance in his holiday photographs were for him stark evidence that he had put on weight in recent years. I asked him whether he had done much swimming before. He told me how he had done a little as a child but considered that he was not very good at it.

IAN: But you had done it before?

GARY: Yes, but not on a regular basis at all. I only went swimming when I went on holiday. It was that type of thing, in for a dip and then come out. But now I go for an hour every day.

IAN: Did you do any swimming at school?

GARY: No, I couldn't really swim that well.

IAN: So you didn't have any instruction or school swimming sessions?

GARY: No, not at all. I used to avoid it.

IAN: What do you mean 'avoid it'?

GARY: Because it was down at the public pool in (local town) and the people who were in my class, I hated a lot of them and a lot of them were bullies – so I decided not to do it.

I was aware from the previous interview that Gary had had a difficult time at school where he had been placed in the lower stream of a large comprehensive. Being placed in the lower stream of this school was considered a double whammy, in that the school was perceived as the place for those who failed the 11+ exam for entry into the nearby grammar school. Within the environment of this school, there appeared to be greater emphasis placed upon overt displays of physicality, whether through sport or acts of aggressive, masculine posturing.

Even though I had asked Gary about how he felt about his body during the previous interview, I ventured the question again.

IAN: How do you think you felt about your own body at that time?

GARY: Oh inadequate. I was really slim, quite thin. I was tall and lanky and I felt quite self-conscious about it.

IAN: Do you think that made more of a difference, your feelings about your body or your ability in terms of comparing yourself with others?

GARY: A bit of both, my ability in swimming – not that well but also, probably my body as well.

IAN: Were the other kids good at swimming?

GARY: Yes some of them were. Some of the bullies were.

The combination of the values within the school placed upon displays of aggressive (hegemonic) masculinity as well as the broader expectation within traditional sports for these performances (Hargreaves 1986, McKay *et al.* 2000, Wellard 2009) and the emphasis upon an ability-centred curriculum in PE (Evans *et al.* 2004) made it increasingly difficult for Gary to engage with school sports activities, let alone enjoy them.

Our conversation moved on to thinking about his relationship with sport and our discussions in the previous interview about tennis and the factors that had contributed to how he chose to continue to take part. (He had not participated at a tennis club during the last ten years but had continued to play with his partner regularly at local public tennis courts. They would rally together and then play friendly sets.) I wanted to find out how he had made a transition from taking up swimming as a direct action to lose weight to how it became an activity that was a regular and important aspect of his life. I was particularly interested in thinking about this in relation to the high drop-out levels of those who take up sport initially where the motivation is relating to losing weight (Trost *et al.* 2002, Whaley and Schrider 2005).

IAN: What was it like the first time you went after you came back from the holiday and had made that resolution to going swimming?

GARY: It was embarrassing really, because I was self-conscious again about the body. I was really overweight and, but when I went into the changing room and I saw other people, older than myself and really big and some even younger than myself and even bigger than me – it gave me a little bit of confidence really.

Gary had decided to take up his swimming regime in a pool in a nearby town. He went for the first time with his partner and although he admitted to having initial doubts he had thought to himself, 'Oh why not' and they ended up swimming that first time for about an hour. I wanted to find out what aspects of that first swim had been enjoyable enough to make him want to continue.

IAN: What can you remember specifically about that first time and what made you want to do it again? If you think about it, there is a big difference between swimming in Greece to swimming in a public pool in England. So what kept your interest?

GARY: I think what kept me… I thought, what I'll try and do is do ten lengths… and I done them and I was exhausted. So I thought I can go back and do 12 lengths next time. And that is what kind of got me started and then I started talking to other people and it became sort of a habit. A lot of the people explained their situation and were there because they wanted to lose weight or get fit. I thought because I was in my forties, I wanted to do something that is low impact, and it's worked.

IAN: Ok, you started and you had a reason for going in the first place, but what do you think has kept you doing it, if you achieved your goal quite some time ago?

GARY: What it is, is when you go swimming and after you really get into it, one thing what swimming does (and it is very important I go in the morning and not in the evening) is it just really sets the day up for you and you come out of that swim and you feel on a high – and you feel ready for the day.

IAN: What do you mean 'getting into it'? How would you describe that to someone who hasn't done it before?

GARY: Um… well, when you, kind of, swim you go into your own world. It's kind of a cross between relaxation and… determination to try and go a little quicker. And if you do lengths, like I do, I like to between 80 and 100 and when you get to that, the determination is to get to 80 and then you think,

'Hold on, I can do another 20 on top of that and it's that determination. It's also about feeling more confident about your body.

What became apparent from Gary's reflections was that swimming allowed him at this stage in his life an opportunity to develop confidence in his own ability. This was a process that needed time and was aided by a range of factors including initial motivation, encouragement from his partner, and an inclusive, unthreatening environment. In this case, the contrast to his experiences in schools sport, especially swimming, is significant. Aside from the unwelcoming social atmosphere generated through the school bullies, it is often the case that school swimming instruction is allocated little time and this time is generally teacher led and skills based (Light and Wallian 2008). The individual agency that Gary relished during his adult venture into swimming allowed him to develop in his own time and at his own pace.

This gradual temporal adjustment had allowed Gary to relax sufficiently to be able to put negative thoughts about his own personal and perceived social identity into the background. Consequently, he was able to 'enjoy' swimming as a time when he could go into his own world. I explained to Gary that this was something that I also found an enjoyable aspect of swimming. I told him that when I went swimming I would 'switch off' and I cherished the opportunity to think about 'things' or even enjoy not having to think about anything except the subconscious motion of my body in the water. I asked Gary how long he thought it had taken for him to get to the stage when he felt confident with his swimming and when he started to go into his 'own world'.

GARY: I'd say it took about a year.
IAN: What makes you stick to an hour session and not pushing to do more lengths?
GARY: No, I find an hour suits me. I find an hour is not exhausting, but… I think you have to find a cut-off point. I could do an hour and a half but I thought, no, it gets ridiculous then. If you are doing it on a daily basis that's seven hours a week and that's quite a lot. If you start doing an hour and a half it is almost like it starts to get out of control. But I think you could fall into that trap if you weren't careful.

Over a period of time Gary had become aware of what suited him and did not feel the need to keep pushing his boundaries or setting further goals as is so often the case in individual sports. At the same time, Gary's reflections demonstrated a form of embodied awareness, or physical literacy (Whitehead 2010) where he had learned to recognise and understand that not every swim would always be the same.

GARY: It is funny really because sometimes you can have good swims and other times bad ones. Cos in that hour you can have a really good swim and do your 100 lengths and it's fantastic and the water is kind of like embracing you in a way. But other times you have your swim for an hour and it can be quite challenging, as in quite difficult.

IAN: So, how do you deal with that?

GARY: Just get through it. Almost go into autopilot. Because I think if I had missed the day and didn't go I would miss it.

Gary's reflections upon the importance of having time to develop an awareness of the swimming resonated with my own thoughts. Even though I did not experience the traumas of school sport in the way that he had, I could empathise with him by remembering that I had learned to swim as a child at my own pace, mainly through the encouragement of my father and opportunities to swim regularly on my own and with friends. School swimming was not a problem for me in the way Gary described because I could, in fact, swim before I started primary school and by the time I was a teenager, the instruction in PE was too basic. However, Gary's experiences of swimming highlight the importance of individual agency. Whereas this may become more complicated within the context of compulsory school education, it is significant within the context of many health-based interventions aimed at adults. In many of these cases, the period of intervention (whether taster sessions or several instruction lessons) is only for a few weeks. If taking into account the time that Gary needed to adapt so that the activity could become relevant and enjoyable, a few weeks is insufficient.

We continued the theme of relevance and I mentioned that I thought it was interesting how it was that swimming had become such a big part of Gary's daily routine. I asked him if there had been any other times in his life when a sport or activity like this had played such a part.

GARY: No, not at all. But I think a main reason is that you get to a certain age and take a look at yourself and think, hang on, if I want to carry on for another 20 years I need to do something about my lifestyle. Cos if I carry on putting on weight and not doing any exercise, I'm not going to... And also looking at those photos of the holiday played a part cos I was thinking, oh god, I want to look a bit sexy and attractive, but how will I look in five or six years if don't do anything? Not just for me but for my partner. And I must say that he has encouraged me as he says I look a lot better now. So this gives you a bit of a buzz, something extra that you get out of it.

IAN: Ok, that makes sense, but what I want to know is what it is about swimming in comparison with other sports. You told me before how you have tried going to the gym and playing tennis. But what is the appeal of swimming apart from that it has helped you lose weight?

GARY: The appeal of swimming for me, probably just for myself, is that swimming, more than any other sport, is manageable. As in, once you start, at first it is difficult, the first month is very difficult cos you want to swim more. Like, if you go for an hour I swim for the whole hour. Some people stop, but I carry on and I think the first month is difficult cos you're trying to increase the number of lengths, but once you've done that it becomes a manageable sport, where you can swim on a daily basis. And the good thing is that you can do it yourself. You don't need a tennis partner. So, even though a lot of people say it must be boring like being in a goldfish bowl where you just swim up and down, but I think it becomes like a state of mind where you think about other things and go into autopilot, and you can't really do that in a lot of other sports.

IAN: Yes, I've always found that difficult to explain to other people. I just seem to switch off and go into my own 'water-world'. But you have also mentioned to me before about the other people and the social side. Is there a social side in any way?

GARY: Yes there is, and I was really surprised because I'm one of these people, I'm quite kind of private. At first I was really quiet because I was conscious of my body, but when you see other people in similar situations, trying to lose weight or get fitter, and then you see some in their seventies going every day – you really admire them. And they're really friendly and encourage you and it's a really good sport for that, and you become friends with them.

IAN: Did the people you became friendly with get into it for similar reasons?

GARY: Yes, some were doing it because they had had injuries and swimming was good because it was low impact. One woman had played a lot of basketball, but had broken her leg and started swimming as a form of non-weight-bearing exercise. She had then, I suppose, like me gotten into it on a regular basis... I think that is another reason why I enjoy swimming is that the injury factor isn't so high and I don't have to worry so much about injuries. I seemed to get a lot when I played tennis, even though I haven't really played that much.

For any recreational sports participant it is more than just 'doing' the activity that determines the overall enjoyment and influences subsequent decisions to continue. Social and physical aspects are just as, if not more, important to the recreational athlete in comparison to the elite or professional. For Gary, not only was the activity manageable in terms of his physical capabilities, it was also something that he could manage at the social level. In our previous interview in 2000 where the focus had been more related to experiences of tennis, Gary had found the pressures to perform, in terms of on-court ability as well as off-court socialising, a significant factor in making the game less enjoyable than he had hoped for.

At this stage, I thought that the conversation had developed enough to change the subject slightly. I wanted to explore further the appeal of swimming and as Gary had mentioned earlier in our conversation that during his 'good swims' the water 'embraced him' I wanted to explore this embodied, pleasurable aspect further.

IAN: Are there any sports that you find sexy?

GARY: Yes – swimming!

IAN: Why is that?

GARY: Because you're naked (laughs). Well it is! You're naked and you cannot help but look at other people's bodies in swimming – and it's probably expected more than any other sport because you are down to your bikini or trunks.

IAN: So is it that? It is sexy because you look at other people or is it sexy being in the water?

GARY: Er, no, I wouldn't say the water is sexy, although sometimes you do feel like you are embraced by the water.

IAN: Yes, that is why I asked this, as you mentioned that earlier.

GARY: Yes, it does sometimes happen. On some occasions you do feel like you could swim forever.

When allowed to consider the broader aspects of the term 'sexy', Gary was able to recognise the embodied, sensual dimensions of swimming that made it attractive and enjoyable for him. Gary also told me that he had become a lot more interested in watching swimming now that he felt he had become more proficient at it. He said that he enjoyed watching swimming races on television in the same way that he liked to watch tennis. He felt that he could associate with these sports more, whereas he would never think of watching any other sport.

Gary's story can be 'read' in terms of his subjective reasoning for taking part in swimming. However, his experiences can also be seen to share similarities with many others in a way that counters arguments suggesting the subjectivity of his accounts are necessarily less meaningful because of their intrinsic nature. The shared meanings allow for consideration of the ways that the social resonates through and beyond the individual.

Elizabeth

I had not interviewed Elizabeth before, and had deliberately focused upon the accounts of men in the previous research on embodied masculinities, for both theoretical and methodological reasons. However, during the fieldwork for that research, and which entailed participating in numerous sports clubs, I was constantly aware of the contrasting experiences of women, who were affected not only by social constructions of gender, but also assumptions related to age and ability.

The experiences of Elizabeth provide an interesting comparison to Gary's accounts in that there are similarities in their decisions to take up sporting activity on a regular basis during middle age. However, there are distinct contrasts in relation to their childhood experiences of sport. Elizabeth did not experience school sport, or school in general, in a negative way, but rather recalls that she was neither good nor bad at sport. Indeed, her reflections highlight the experiences of many in that she considered herself 'invisible' in many aspects of school life and this invisibility was something she often consciously aimed for.

Elizabeth recalled her early experiences of sport, describing herself as being 'not sporty'. For her and her family, music was the main activity. She played the violin as a child and, for her, this was considered to be her 'sport'. Her parents were both teachers. Her father was a geography teacher and her mother had taught until Elizabeth's older sister was born.

ELIZABETH: In terms of activities, my parents did a lot of walking and rambling. Lots of activities based around this. They wouldn't have seen it as sport, but it was obviously a recreational activity.

IAN: What do you remember about doing these activities with your parents?

ELIZABETH: Quite sort of regimented. Quite sort of focused, like, 'Right, we're going to do 16 miles today.' It was sort of trudging. I enjoyed it, but I didn't know anything different.

Elizabeth explained that her father was a geography teacher and that his interests in natural geography extended beyond the classroom and influenced the choices the family made in leisure activities. She recalled how as a young child she would often accompany her father and his sixth-form students on field trips to Snowdonia. Consequently, her recollections of family activities were dominated by trips to historic sites and National Trust areas. Elizabeth summarised these activities as 'heritage things and picnics', with her father's central philosophy being that of the family doing things together.

ELIZABETH: It was that you don't need to spend a lot of money. He was very financially orientated even though they were financially well off... Our family enjoyment came from being together and always these involved doing lots of walking and looking at things. And probably even when I was too young, as I can remember when I was really young being bored doing certain things, although I wasn't bored to the point that I didn't want to do it again.

IAN: But I suppose it is like you say, you didn't know any different.

ELIZABETH: No, I just remember lots of damp weather and, you know, you'd be out in it no matter what is going on. That is what we did until I was about nine or ten, and then my parents started taking us abroad.

By the time Elizabeth had reached her teens, the family were venturing further afield and taking trips to Europe. At this stage, Elizabeth commented that she felt it was interesting that as she got older she became more interested in travel and how this had obviously played a significant part in her later career path. At the same time, she noticed how her walking experiences with her family had also influenced the way she conducted her own leisure activities with her children.

ELIZABETH: Yes, and walking is an activity now with my children. As soon as they could toddle, I got them walking everywhere. They will walk miles now. They are six and a half now and they will walk about eight or nine miles on a day's walk.

IAN: It's been interesting during this research how it has made me reflect upon some of the key things in my early days that have stayed with me.

ELIZABETH: It's quite amusing the thing about walking and being in Wales in the bad weather. My friend who lives in the north-west of England has a caravan there [in Wales] and she's starting to do that with her children in the way that our parents did with us – so it resonates.

Whereas Elizabeth's recollections of family activities were remembered fondly, within the context of school sport, her memories were less affectionate. Her most vivid recollections of school sport related to swimming.

ELIZABETH: As soon as we started doing swimming at school, I hated it. I absolutely loathed it.

IAN: Why was that?

ELIZABETH: A mixture of things. I wasn't a strong swimmer and we had a pool at the school. Because my dad taught there, I'd go swimming with my dad and my sister. So all my teachers were there with their children and I just found that a bit bizarre, almost embarrassing. But it was swimming in PE with Mrs S, I can remember her clearly. She used to make us thrash up and down the pool until we dropped dead basically. And I almost did once. They thought I had epilepsy as I kind of blacked out, not a fit but a sort of blackout. So my early memories of swimming are not good ones at all.

IAN: Did you learn to swim at school?

ELIZABETH: I was taught to swim by my dad in a different swimming pool and probably quite badly in fact. Then at school it seemed to me to be more about bodies rather than values. Doing as much as you could and doing bronze, silver and gold and getting a brick [from the bottom of the pool]. But I just found it very unpleasant and not enjoyable. There were a couple of kids who were great, doing all the galas, but everybody else didn't like it.

IAN: It's strange in a lot of schools that there seems to be a fear sometimes kids are going to enjoy swimming and that they shouldn't; where the idea that splashing around and enjoying being in the pool is not 'proper' in the context of PE.

ELIZABETH: Exactly, it was more severe, more strict than any other sport we did or any other lessons. Tennis was a bit like that. We didn't do much tennis, but when we did it was spoilt because it was very strictly taught. You couldn't have a go at just backwards and forwards, you had to do it a certain way. You know that from about the age of 12, 13 I never went swimming until I was about 21. I had absolutely no desire to go during that time. And when I finally did, it was because some of my friends decided to go at university and I went along. It's strange, because the only other thing I can remember about swimming is that we had a pool at my primary school, but we only seemed to ever go in it when it was a gala. Then we would be all perched along the side, go in for a bit and then come out. I can remember it being freezing and traumatic. You had to change out in the open air and it was all just very horrible and not enjoyable.

At this point, I mentioned how it seemed ironic that adults sometimes forget that children do actually have physical sensations and emotions. They do feel the cold and feel exposed both literally and psychologically. Elizabeth agreed:

ELIZABETH: No, I know. It's like the netball and hockey. Mrs S, same teacher again, whistle, layered up to the elbows, mug of coffee and I was running about with a little Airtex top and skirt in the freezing cold. It's terrible thinking about it now and hating every minute of it.

I could empathise with Elizabeth and the indignation that she felt having to run around in the freezing cold while wearing inadequate clothing. I have mentioned elsewhere (2009) that, as a child, after returning from the warm climate of Australia I was horrified at having to play football in English winter time. I can still remember (and feel) the pain of a football smacking against my shivering body. At that time, I was also aware of what I considered to be the injustice of the situation in that there appeared absolutely no question in the PE teacher's mind other than that we were doing this because it was 'good' for us. In that context, I had talked about my experiences in terms of how an 'expected' form of masculinity was reinforced. However, both Elizabeth's and my recollections were not just about gender, they were also about an embodied sensibility performed by the PE teachers developed through understandings of gender as well as the social perceptions they held relating to their own experiences of sport and the unquestioned benefits that taking part would deliver.

At this stage, I asked Elizabeth whether she could remember any of the activities that she considered 'fun' when she was a teenager. She described how she started to do some running when she was about 15. Some of her friends had taken it up, and one of the activities that she remembered in particular was an even called 'night-pilot' which was a form of orienteering at night. Her friends, including her boyfriend at the time, set up a team so that they could enter these locally organised competitions. However, the appeal was more related to being out with her friends all night.

ELIZABETH: When I think about it now, I don't know how my parents let me do it. So we'd go off. It was run by some private company. You'd register your team and you'd go on practice night-pilots. You'd have maps and head torches and you'd go out into the woods and you follow a track round and then there was one big competition in the summer after exams – and so you had to get fit for that – cos we'd basically be out all night roaming around these woods. It was about five miles.
IAN: So you hadn't done any running before this?
ELIZABETH: No, only in as much as at school. When we did do cross-country I was ok at that. Not because I was a great runner, but I was a bit of a slogger. I would get there. So we did this night-pilot training throughout my fifth year at secondary. That was for about six or seven months and then I stopped running. But at that time there wasn't much else for us to do. A friend and

I would run from my house to another friend's house and have a cup of tea which was about five miles away. At the time, although we didn't really think much of it, I did feel real satisfaction in being able to run all the way there without stopping. So, now when I run, I can really relate to that sense of satisfaction when I do a 10k. It is interesting thinking about it, because I can remember thinking, 'If I can get to the church, I can get to the village hall,' and to the next bit and so on. And I do that now when I run, I set myself targets.

For Elizabeth, much of her participation in sporting activities was instigated by others. She took part to be with her friends, and the activities were more relevant because they allowed her to be with friends. She did not take part in any sporting activities while at university and this was because there were many other forms of activity that she could take part in with friends. She did a lot of travelling, but no sport. It was not until after university (when she started another relationship) that she became involved in mountaineering and outdoor walking. It was an activity that her boyfriend was already heavily into and Elizabeth followed suit. I asked whether this was driven by him and she said that it was completely so.

ELIZABETH: It was definitely driven by him and I think he was pleasantly surprised that he was with somebody who would do all of that with him.
IAN: And you enjoyed doing that?
ELIZABETH: Yes
IAN: What did you like about it?
ELIZABETH: It was quite risky and it pushed me to the limits of my – of what I thought I could do and what was comfortable. You know, you'd be up a peak and you'd be slipping around with crampons and ropes around you. So it was quite, not dangerous, but with an element of risk. Whereas walking around with the family as a child was pretty safe.
IAN: I suppose that being with a partner there was an element of trust
ELIZABETH: (overlapping) Yes, yes
IAN: and that must be nice for a relationship.
ELIZABETH: Yes because within a few months of us meeting we walked the West Highland Way, we did it as a kind of race against some friends who ended up copping out after a couple of days. It rained and it snowed and we carried all our stuff with us and we camped out. And to do that with someone I didn't really know, that worked well.

I asked how the race came about and Elizabeth explained that it started out as a conversation in a pub which ended up with the other couple saying that they could probably do the walk more quickly than the time Elizabeth and her partner had said would be a reasonable time to do it in. She continued taking part in mountaineering and hill walking all the while she was with this boyfriend (about five years). After they split up, Elizabeth did not do it any more. She said that she would not have continued it on her own and that it was not such a big part of her life in maybe the way it was for him. In addition she moved location for a new job and the focus changed.

When she started her new job, she told me that she did not take part in anything sports related for several years until 'out of the blue' she started to go swimming. When I asked her why this was, she could not recall any direct reason. I ventured that it might have made more sense for her to go running, given her previous dislike for swimming. Elizabeth felt that even though she was not entirely sure, it was more likely that an opportunity arose and it gave her the chance to prove to herself that she could do it. This lasted for about three years during which time she would go regularly before work. I suggested that maybe because she had been able to start swimming on her own terms it meant she could do what she wanted and get out whenever she wanted. Interestingly, Elizabeth explained that every time she went she would swim for precisely 40 minutes.

ELIZABETH: But I always did exactly 40 minutes, not a minute less or a minute more. I have no idea why it became 40 minutes. But maybe the logic behind it was that half an hour wasn't quite enough and you'd made all the effort to come down, so 40 minutes seemed more reasonable.

It also seemed that the timing (getting changed and the swim) was manageable before work. The swimming stopped when she met her husband and then soon had children. For about ten years she did not participate in any sporting activities. At the time of the interview, Elizabeth had only started running a year and a half ago. Taking up running had also coincided with her separation from her husband. At this point, we were then able to reflect upon the different factors that contributed to her taking part in these activities both now and previously. The social element was a significant factor, but Elizabeth also admitted that the competitive edge was another. Not necessarily in terms of a quest for trophies, but rather as something that gave the activity more of an edge and a focus. Consequently, when she did take up running, she explained how it was not until she joined a group (a running club) with a little element of competition and targets that she got into it in a bigger way.

ELIZABETH: When I started to run on my own it wasn't enough to really compel me, to make me get better and faster. Even though the group I go with is a really friendly and probably non-competitive club, it made me start to set more targets about where I wanted to be.
IAN: Yes and it gives you a bit more discipline. It's like I'll go to the gym because I will focus more rather than if I did it at home.
ELIZABETH: Yeah when I run on my own, I don't do as much. Whereas when you're with a running club you pretty much go and you don't stop and just do what you set out to do.
IAN: So how did this sudden take up of running on a serious basis start for you?
ELIZABETH: A colleague (Sally) who started working directly with me, she started about three years ago. And I was aware that she 'ran' although I didn't

talk to her a lot about it at first as I didn't know her that well, but I knew she'd done a marathon somewhere along the line

IAN: What did you think about that at the time?

ELIZABETH: I thought 'Wow, that's amazing' and cos both of us are the same age and she clearly is fit and she never gets ill – and I'm terrible for coughs and throats and colds. But that was on my mind. So, for a period of about 18 months, she would be saying, 'Why don't you just go out and run? – I'll come with you if you want.' So it was about January 2010, I got on some electronic scales and I was 11and a half stone and I was weighing the same as I did when I had my twins. The combination of that and the conversations with Sally gradually saying why don't you just and that I weighed as much as when I had two babies inside me – when I should be about nine and a half stone – made up my mind. I literally went out the next day to the running shop and spent £100 on a pair of top-level running shoes (laughs) – you know, like when you make up your mind you've got to do it now. So I bought the kit and that day I went out of the house and said, 'I'm going to start my running today.' It was the 2nd of January. I ran, I kid you not (points out) from about here to that building there (about 25 metres) (laughs) and was gasping, and I staggered around our estate which is about point-eight of a mile and it was just like having a heart attack when I got back. But I was so pleased with myself and I just kept doing that. Point-eight of a mile for a couple of weeks and then a mile and a half.

IAN: But it was good you did that.

ELIZABETH: Yes, I was kind of so psyched and so many people said to me, 'Saw you running today,' (emphasised the way that they said it in a curious fashion) – meaning that I must have looked awful.

IAN: So why did you do that? Rather than go to a gym and run on a treadmill or go swimming again?

ELIZABETH: I did remember about the night-pilot thing and that I had enjoyed it and I wasn't bad at it. But Sally as well was a big influence on me. She told me so many funny stories about running with her friends, and, you know, it's cheap. We don't have a lot of disposable income. And the ease of it – you can have your tea, put the kids to bed and just go. That first four weeks was the make or break and in Jan in the hideous weather. But about after six weeks, the first time I ran with Sally I could see that she was shocked about how unfit I still was with any slight incline. So I found that quite difficult, her seeing how difficult I found it, but she was so good and so encouraging and she continued to go out with me every week and basically go at half her pace to get me going. She got me doing two miles, three miles, four miles. Got me to the point where I could run a local 10k in May, albeit in an hour and a quarter. And right up until that September when I did the half [marathon]. She basically coached me all through that summer and got me up to doing ten miles – to the extent where I think she actually affected her own performance. She under-ran when we did the half marathon and I've always felt that it was such a good thing to do for someone else, cos that meant I stuck with it, and I've stuck with it since then.

Elizabeth felt that there had been a period when the running had become almost an obsession, but now felt that this obsessive approach had peaked and she was returning to a level, running twice a week, which was both comfortable for her and manageable. I asked her why she thought that her running had become obsessive and she explained that the preparation for a marathon took far more time that she had envisaged. However, an underlying factor in the amount of time that she devoted to the training was the personal element. She told me that once she had made up her mind to enter the marathon she was determined to see it through, regardless of how much preparation she needed and how long it took her to do the race. This determination was also fuelled by her harbouring what she considered a 'chip on her shoulder' about proving to others that she could do things that she felt they did not believe she could achieve or see through.

I wondered whether her recollections of feeling somewhat 'invisible' during her school days had any bearing on this frame of mind and she agreed that it was a contributing factor to her 'chip on her shoulder' about not being recognised as a child and that she was never thought of as sporty, or would ever be.

Elizabeth's feelings of unworthiness in relation to sport aligned with a sense of indignation about how others viewed her ability resonates with the responses of many of the men I interviewed who played tennis and had had negative experiences of school sport (Wellard 2009). Just like Elizabeth, there was acknowledgement that some aspects of their participation as adults related to attempts to prove to themselves as well as to others that they could in fact be successful in a sport. Ultimately, this determination also placed additional pressure to achieve more tangible evidence of success. Whereas, for the men who played tennis, achievement was acknowledged through winning matches, for Elizabeth the focus was upon the times taken to run her races.

ELIZABETH: Yes, it's strange, because it's like with the 10k – I was still disappointed with my performance and I expected to do better. And there were several from work at the finish line who had come to support and I was disappointed because they were seeing me this way rather than what I knew I could do.

IAN: It's interesting also that if you think about when you first started and how far you've come – but you are still disappointed and have also become fixed on the time as a measure of your performance. When do you think the focus on times came about?

ELIZABETH: I think the time thing was inevitable. As soon as you do enter a race, people say to you, 'How long is it going to take you?' When I did my first race, I remember Sally had told me that the first time she had done it, it took her 1hour and 5 minutes. I thought I'd aim for an hour and 5 and I did 1 hour 15 and I was devastated, but then again there were a lot of people coming in behind me. Then I did another and came in at 1.13 and then another at 1.12

and then the last one I did, I got down to 1.06 and there was no one there to see me (laughs). But then this year I thought I would do it in an hour and I did 1.08 and I was so disappointed, but I think I was still weary from the marathon. But it is funny because others are not that interested. No one has asked me the time I did for the marathon. It is much more a personal thing – and I feel that I have achieved what I set out to do in that I have got 'fitter'.

In less than two years, Elizabeth had come a long way in terms of her running. She had started as a novice and developed to the stage where she could take part in 10-kilometre runs and even marathons. During this time, it was apparent that the ways in which she experienced running had transformed. She had learned to 'think' like a runner in that her orientation to the activity had moved from that of being able to run a certain distance, such as twice around her estate, to setting times for her runs and getting to know how her body would respond at particular stages of a 10k race. Bearing in mind this notion of transformation, I wanted to find out whether Elizabeth was aware of any changes in the way that she 'enjoyed' running. I asked her directly what she considered to be the most enjoyable aspect of running a marathon.

ELIZABETH: Talking to people about doing it and talking about the training. Talking about the process of the training and what races I was going to do leading up to it. The planning for it and the planning for all the running for that amount of time. Actually running it was hell. I can honestly say I did not enjoy the run itself. It was the 'whole' thing. Even getting across the finish line, there wasn't that 'ARRH, I've done it'. I felt more jubilant finishing the 10k.

Like Jodie and Nick in the previous chapter, taking part in running events was, for Elizabeth, one aspect of the 'whole package' of sport (Wellard 2002). In the same way as she had taken part in the 'night-pilot' event as a teenager, the marathon was much more to Elizabeth than just a running event. It provided opportunities for her to engage with the sport at personal, social and physical levels. At the same time, the way that Elizabeth described how she did not enjoy the actual run highlights the ways in which, like accounts of professional athletes, many aspects of sport involve experiencing pain. Indeed, in some cases, enjoyment becomes coterminous with pain where it is not possible to experience the pleasurable aspects after the event without experiencing physical pain during the activity.

We talked about the complexity of explaining pain and how, in some activities, such as aerobics, there might be pain that can be experienced as enjoyable both before and after. However, Elizabeth graphically described the latter stages of the marathon in terms of pain rather than any form of pleasure.

ELIZABETH: I can honestly say that in the last three miles I felt like someone had a knife and they were dragging it up and down my legs. That's the only way I can describe it. They were so painful and so heavy, I just felt like… I did feel like they were going to fall off. The pain was so intense and I was so tired.

IAN: So why didn't you stop?

ELIZABETH: I'd run 23 miles, I had three miles left to do. It's three and a half times round my estate. I did visualise it in that way.

IAN: So in some way, all the other stuff surrounding the marathon and your build up to it is almost overriding the pain.

ELIZABETH: And the thought of finishing, or not finishing it and going back in the car with the girls, with me finishing at 23 – no, that just wasn't going to happen. Short of me collapsing in the heat, there was no way I wasn't going to finish it.

Fun, but more than fun

Elizabeth's description of the agonies she endured in the last stages of her marathon resonates with many other competitors in such races. By competing in an organised marathon, Elizabeth also had to negotiate the prevailing discourses that have shaped the contemporary understanding of what taking part entails. In this case, the marathon is not only part of the broader 'institution' of sport, but could be considered to have become an institution in its own right. However, part of the social construction of an institution is the discourse it generates and how knowledge permeates into everyday (uncritical) practice. The prevailing message is that, taking part in a marathon and, importantly, finishing ascribes 'certain attributes, qualities and even character' (Ahmed 2010: 104) upon the runner. Consequently, Elizabeth was not only fearful of letting down her friends, but also the charity that she was collecting money for as part of competing in the marathon. The recent popularity of running has coincided with the expectation that larger races will inevitably involve entrants running on behalf of a particular charity (Nettleton and Hardey 2006). For instance, television coverage of the 2012 London Marathon incorporated many short interviews with competitors, both elite and 'fun' runners (media terms for distinguishing between the serious sports performer and the worthy amateur). During filming of the race, many of the fun-runners were interviewed before, during and after the races. On many occasions, interviewers, positioned at various stages throughout the course would stop runners to ask them either how they were getting on or, more importantly, who they were *running for*. Indeed, the prevailing message was that the fun-runners were not running for selfish, personal reasons, but had more altruistic motivations.

In many of the post-match interviews the fun-runners described the physical agonies of running in detail, but when asked why they continued to run despite the pain, their responses were that they were doing it not only for themselves, but for others. These 'others' were generally friends and relatives who had a health-related story (Nettleton and Hardey 2006) and the charity they were running to raise money for was linked to the specific illness or condition central to their story.

Resilience

Gary and Elizabeth, just like Jodie and Nick in the previous chapter, displayed forms of resilience in the way that they have been able to participate in sports despite their negative experiences during their schooldays. Elizabeth Hoult, in her study of resilience in adult learners suggests that resilience emerges as a result of

> complex interactions between the learner and his or her context and is therefore neither entirely innate to the learner, nor is it the direct result of strategies 'outside' of the learner.
>
> (Hoult 2009: 250)

Here, Hoult's focus is on the ways that adult learners have been able to participate successfully in education in later life after having been unsuccessful (in terms of educational achievement) in their compulsory years of school-based education. There are similarities within the context of sport and the ways that both Gary and Elizabeth could be considered 'unsuccessful' (learners in sport) in relation to their achievements in school-based sports activities. However, their resilience can be seen in the way that they have persevered with attempts to engage with sport as adults despite their perceived identities (both personal and social) as being 'non-sporty'.

In the interviews that Hoult conducted with adult learners, she found that a significant part of the process of resilience was that learners engaged in 'plural and open' readings and resisted 'closed meanings' (2009: 251). In the context of education, this meant challenging authoritative readings of texts and also challenging authoritative readings of themselves as texts. Consequently, the authoritative narratives that emanated from Elizabeth's and Gary's teachers and throughout their experiences of school sport were based upon perceptions of ability and classifications (by the PE teachers and students) of who was considered more appropriate to take part. Similarly, within the context of 'sport' in its traditional form, the 'market segments' identified by Sport England (see Chapter 2) can be seen to reinforce restricted interpretations of the sportsperson.

Gary and Elizabeth, as well as Jodie and Nick, can be seen to resist the closed readings that Hoult describes and they also reject those readings of themselves. For instance, Elizabeth can be seen to resist the narrow categorisation of 'middle-aged woman' that the specific Sport England segments identify as encapsulating the sporting identity of a woman her age. Hoult suggests that

> Resilient learners show a willingness to divest themselves of their 'clothing' (inherited ways of thinking and externally imposed identities) and they try on new clothes.
>
> (Hoult 2009: 253)

Gary and Elizabeth draw upon a range of narratives to justify and continue their participation. It might be the case that their perceptions of 'outsiderness' realised in relation to traditional constructions of the sporting participant have presented Gary and Elizabeth with a form of liberation in older age and this has allowed them to find an activity that works for them and one that they enjoy.

6 Personal reflections and shared stories

Undergraduate days at university might be best described as a time when my eyes were opened to viewing the world with a sociological lens as well as a time when I realised what it was that I enjoyed most about tennis. It might be accurate to say that the degree I obtained was unofficially one in Sociology and tennis. Playing tennis during that time rekindled the joy that I had found in it as a child but which had diminished somewhat during my teens when I had been involved in competitive, ratings tournaments. As a child, I had loved going to the park with a friend and just hitting the ball for hours. Sometimes we would play sets, but most of the time we would just hit the ball endlessly. My memories now are of long hot summer days when we would take packed lunches with us so that we did not have to interrupt our sessions by needing to return home, even though we lived only a couple of minutes away.

What I was able to capture again at university was the joy in playing tennis with friends and being part of a team. In particular, I had a couple of friends who were tennis 'buddies' in that they felt the same as me about playing and would want to do so whenever possible. There were some old tarmac tennis courts at the back of the main building where we could play after lectures. However, we all preferred, if we had the time, to make the trip to the university sports ground, which was situated in a quiet suburb on the outskirts of the city. The grounds were at one time the halls of residence but these had been sold off to become an imposing retirement home. The university still owned the grounds, about several acres, and facilities on them included cricket, football and rugby pitches and a large clubhouse with a bar and changing rooms. Most importantly for us, though, there were six tennis courts positioned at the far end of the fields, in a secluded position behind the retirement home. Many times as I walked past the building to get to the courts there were groups of elderly men and women sitting outside enjoying the fresh air and, possibly, being entertained by the sporting activities going on in the grounds.

The courts were always available and we made the most of any opportunities to get down there. We were all part of the university team and would

take part in practice sessions there, as well as matches with other univer-
sities or other clubs in regional leagues. However, we all enjoyed far more
our own trips down there as it meant we could just 'hit' the ball for hours.
We all had similar stories to tell about playing with friends in the park as
youngsters and shared the same pleasure in being able to recapture some
of those childhood memories by playing together. Simple things like being
able to play tennis without our shirts on during the summer months made the
experiences less like formal matches or sessions at the clubs we belonged
to outside university. A shared 'understanding' of tennis also made playing
the competitive matches in the university team additionally enjoyable. Our
mutual love of playing tennis was built upon a sense of wanting to 'enjoy'
playing rather than necessarily considering winning as the ultimate goal.

During those times, there was an intimacy that developed between us in the
way that we recognised that what we were experiencing, at a personal level,
when playing tennis was felt in a similar way by the others. Consequently,
during those sessions, because we knew each other so well we did not have to
worry about anything else and could just hit the ball (what seemed like) for
ever, enjoy being in the sun and relish our time together. Indeed, our regular
forays to play tennis at those courts made the team even stronger in that we
all approached the game with a similar mindset.

Throughout this book, I have attempted to incorporate a reflective approach
to the consideration of fun and enjoyment in sport. My research background
is located within what could be considered traditional sociology and this has
informed my approach to empirical fieldwork. In most cases this has entailed the
use of life-history techniques similar to those of Plummer (1983) and Connell
(2005) collected through ethnographic fieldwork. Much of this approach to
collecting data has been governed by an understanding that 'other' people are
the focus of the research. Consequently, my ethnographic strategy has been a
constant attempt to 'fit in' with the groups of people that I am studying and not
to draw attention to myself as a researcher; in other words, deflect attention
from myself and make attempts at what Silverman (1989) describes as 'cautious
positivism'.

This approach has not, however, ignored the importance of the subjective
and has constantly acknowledged the reflexive processes at play throughout any
forms of research (Bourdieu and Wacquant 1992) as well as the implications of
co-construction during interviews (Kvale 1996). However, because I have been
grappling with issues relating to the embodied self and the ways in which the
body is contemplated in a multidimensional corporeal sense, reflective processes
have become more prominent and, as such, I have felt a greater need to consider
the relevance of my own self within research and the formulation of theory. As
Knowles and Gilbourne (2010) suggest, critical social science encourages an
understanding of the self in a wider-world context and through an approach such
as auto-ethnography, requiring the author to engage with varying degrees of
reflection.

Consequently, in an attempt to step a little outside my theoretical and methodological comfort zones and question further some of the issues relating to sport, fun and enjoyment, I have attempted to apply a personal lens to my existing techniques. I would imagine, however, to the seasoned auto-ethnographer, my attempts would be considered as that of a novice. Nevertheless, the purpose throughout has been an attempt to focus a wider lens on existing 'tried and tested' techniques and reflect upon the 'personal' within research processes.

To an extent, I have already included a variety of methodological approaches to qualitative research within this book. However, in this chapter, I incorporate elements of more established retrospective ethnographic procedures (Sparkes 2002), as well as contemplating experience as it occurs by acknowledging both emotional ethnography (Owen 2006) and experiential ethnography (Weed 2006) so that a broader 'embodied ethnography' can be considered. In doing so, I have also applied a critical, reflective process through the concept of body-reflexive pleasures, described in Chapter 2, which draws upon Connell's (2005) concept of body-reflexive practices. The intention for utilising such techniques is to incorporate a form of 'embodied ontology' where experience is inextricably linked to individual contemplation of a body that is shaped through a consciousness of the presence of others.

In Chapter 2, I described my memory bank of stored pleasurable 'moments' that I had experienced playing tennis. These memories are acknowledged as being subjective and personal, but, at the same time, many aspects of them are, I suggest, familiar to and experienced by others. Therefore, I am also arguing throughout this book that constant reflection upon what does, indeed, make an experience of sport 'fun' is continually being assessed and renegotiated. It may be the case, however, that for those with lower 'reserves' of pleasurable memories, these reflections become more crucial in determining future participation in contrast to a seasoned sports player with an extensive history of sport participation.

In the first two chapters, I also provided examples from my early childhood memories of swimming. These were exciting times and they provide me with happy memories of activities that reverberated with sensations of eager anticipation, physical thrills and personal experiences, all of which have influenced the way that I approach sport and physical activity as an adult. Writing this book now, as a middle-aged adult, I still find swimming enjoyable, but the extent to which I am able to participate has been affected by a range of factors. I am less likely to get the urge to throw myself off a cliff into the sea or do a 'massive bomb' in the local swimming pool. However, I can still understand the sense of thrill that actions like these can produce. Much of my hesitance to do this now is related to the physical changes in my body and the assessment that I would have to make relating to whether my physical body would be able to 'cope' with the consequences of such actions. Consequently, a judgement of how I am actually feeling (physically) at the time is now a major consideration in deciding upon the action to take. Questions such as, 'Do I have a headache? Is one likely? Is my shoulder sore from tennis yesterday?' and a range of others become part of the process prior to swimming now, as I know that, if my physiological condition is not 'right' at the particular moment, I will not enjoy the activity in the way that I want to and will most likely suffer the (health-related) consequences afterwards.

As I have grown older, I have got to 'know' my body. There are days when it does not feel so good, and other days when I feel extremely healthy. I can tell the signs. These physiological changes happen to everyone. I am not unique. We all have to live with our bodies. However, what have also changed, more significantly during the ageing process, are the social factors that influence the ways that I can express my body in the context of swimming (as well as other sports). So, if I were to have a day when I felt extremely healthy and had an urge to relive those childhood experiences, it would be more likely that my awareness of the probable negative social reaction to a middle-aged man, on his own, doing a massive bomb in the local pool would quell any such thoughts.

To reiterate a point made above, to the seasoned auto-ethnographer, my reflections are probably less 'revealing' than would be expected within the context of a robust auto-ethnography. However, within the context of my research background and the aims of this book, as well as in my attempts to draw upon personal reflections of childhood sport, what I have found revealing was my unease (or reluctance) to write about myself. In previous work it has felt more 'natural' to describe a situation and comment upon processes from an observational perspective, but more problematic to talk about myself. It felt that turning the spotlight upon myself deflected attention from what I should be looking at. In other words, my understanding of my training as a researcher has been to act as the 'eyes' of the reader, and because of this I have concentrated upon telling and interpreting what I saw rather than describing how 'I' felt. My feelings were to be directed towards consideration of the questions and themes in the research. Consequently, the focus in this book has been to make attempts to shift from disembodied theorising to incorporating research that literally discloses the personal. Accommodating an inward gaze has forced me to think about myself in the social world, more than in previous research and, in consequence, look at experience from an individual perspective. I did not find it particularly easy to place myself under the lens and maybe this can be explained, in part, by my sociological background where it is easier to investigate or 'reveal' the lives of other people. Indeed, as is the case with adopting an inward gaze, it was not always easy confronting aspects of one's own identity.

What follows are two personal 'reflections' relating to previous and current sporting experience. They are intended as a stimulus for thinking about the range of personal, physical and social elements that contribute to an experience. Importantly, reflection upon particular memories allows a way of looking at the broader dimensions relating to time, spaces and the development of an orientation towards (or not) an activity. In both cases, as a child and as an adult, the role of enjoyment is central to continued participation. Enjoyment is multidimensional, and the ways that an activity is experienced as fun are not necessarily the same on every occasion. These reflections are offered as a means to consider the merits of subjective interpretations of an activity and possibly encourage further debate about the implications that subjective experience has upon childhood and adult recreational sport participation.

Reflections in the water

> As a teenager, when my parents decided to return to England, I went to a
> local secondary school. My experiences of sport in Australia were mostly
> enjoyable. The memory that I relate in Chapter 2 about jumping off the rocks
> into the sea was fairly typical. Swimming was a large part of my life, at
> school and in leisure time. Tennis occupied other times and school PE was
> relatively uneventful.
>
> When I arrived at the school in England, it was in the middle of winter at
> the start of the new term in January. The dominant sport, or what appeared
> to me to be the only sport played, was football. I had no previous experience
> playing it and my skills were 'rubbish' in comparison with those of the other
> boys in my year. My only option was to become 'invisible' during PE lessons.
> I had realised that I could never catch up with the football skills of the 'good'
> ones but I did not want to be grouped with the boys that the PE teachers
> had clearly classified as 'beyond hope'. There was no hiding the fact that
> the PE teachers had their favourites, those being the boys who played
> for the school team. I noticed that there was a different way the teachers
> engaged with them. They would talk about school matches and professional
> football matches. There would sometimes be what appeared friendly banter.
> Although it could be argued that there is nothing wrong with this, it was in
> stark contrast to the way that the teachers communicated with the rest of the
> group. For us it was instructions, commands and orders. I can remember
> being aware of this at the time as I it was not something that I had noticed in
> other subjects.
>
> In the summer of that first year, the school had its annual sports day. The
> event was organised around a series of sporting competitions between the
> four school 'houses'. One of the events was a swimming gala that was to be
> held at the local pool. It was arranged that each year group would attend,
> en masse, at a set time during the day to watch the races and support their
> house. A few weeks before the sports day, there had been invitations from
> the house leaders for volunteers to compete in the races. The school did not
> have any tradition in swimming, with only very occasional trips to the local
> pool made as part of PE requirements to provide some form of instruction.
> Not surprisingly, there were not that many students who turned up to the
> trial session. During this session, I informed the coordinator that I had
> swam quite a lot before and without much deliberation I was entered for the
> 100m freestyle and the relay. For some reason that I could not explain, all
> the good football boys were in another house. It might have been a coinci-
> dence that the house they were in was led by the head of PE; I hadn't really
> thought anything of it at the time. I subsequently found out that several of
> them had entered for the races as well. Apart from being an opportunity to
> swim, which I enjoyed, taking part also meant that I wouldn't have to risk
> being placed randomly in another sports day event on the school field. These
> events were organised by the PE staff and I had been told by friends that

they invariably involved mini five-a-side football tournaments and penalty shoot-out competitions.

It was exciting going to the pool on the sports day. Several buses had been laid on to transport the whole year group for our events, which were held in the morning. I felt a thrill of anticipation that I was going to take part in the event. I cannot remember feeling worried in any way about winning or losing. I knew that I could swim reasonably well and as I didn't know what the others were like, it was hard to know exactly what to expect. I did have concerns about diving from starting blocks and was slightly worried that I hadn't had enough practice and that I might miss the dive and either do a belly-flop or hit the bottom of the pool – in front of the whole year group.

There was a noticeable 'buzz' in the air. The atmosphere was enhanced as the pool had only a relatively small viewing area. This meant the students were packed into tight rows at the sides and far end of the pool. Consequently, the noise of excited children– who were not necessarily bothered about the forthcoming races, but revelling in being outside school with their friends– combined with the packed-in bodies and the acoustics of the swimming pool meant that the noise within the building was electrifying. However, when the races started, the spectators seemed to become even more excited and I was surprised by the extent to which they became involved in cheering on their houses. By this stage, the event had developed into something much more than I had expected. The increased noise and excitement made me more excited too, as well as nervous. But it was nervousness that I understood as thrilling and enjoyable, rather than foreboding.

When my first race was called, I went up to the starting blocks and had a brief moment to soak up the atmosphere. I could see the spectators along the sides and at the far end. I couldn't recognise any faces as it was hard to stop and focus as my eyes panned around the scene. The water looked calm and I remembered my Saturday morning trips to the public pool with my Dad. There was part of me that wanted to do a massive bomb at that very moment, but I knew it wasn't the right time. I think I even worked out at that stage the consequences of doing it. My 'street' credibility among my peers would have soared, but at the same time, I knew that I didn't crave that and the extra negative attention from teachers was not worth it. At that moment, any subversive thoughts were put to one side when I noticed that one of the good football boys was swimming in the lane next to me. There was no rivalry between us at a personal level. He did not know me as I was not one of his football buddies and the only time our paths crossed was when larger groups were merged for PE. In those cases, however, there was streaming in relation to ability and I was always placed in the anonymous middle group that the PE teachers had determined to be neither good nor 'no-hopers'. He wasn't a bully and didn't appear to readily exploit the obvious status he had accrued through his football success and relationship with the PE staff. There was, however, a distinct air of arrogance about him. He expected to win and I imagine his house leader (the head of PE) expected the same.

Our names and the houses we were representing were announced over the speaker while we waited on the blocks. It was disconcerting having my name called out and I wasn't sure whether I enjoyed the brief focus of attention. There was a louder cheer when the football boy's name was called out and I noticed several of his football friends in a group along the side.

There was a moment of silence as we took our starting positions. I heard the starter pistol fire and launched myself forward towards the still water. It was like doing a massive bomb, as I could feel the water explode around me. The football boy had set off at a break-neck speed and I could sense him creating what seemed like enormous waves ahead of me. I thought at that stage, 'He cannot possibly keep that up for four lengths (of the 25-metre pool), but if he does, then he deserves to win.' I decided it was pointless trying to catch up with him as it would mean disrupting the rhythm that I wanted to get into. So I concentrated on getting into my stroke and gradually increasing the pace. My initial instincts were right and by the second lap I had caught him up. On my glimpses of him as I took a breath I could see that his arms were flailing more than necessary and he was tiring. I continued at my pace and by the third length I was some distance ahead of football boy and the others, a few of whom were starting to catch him too. Turning into the last length I knew that I would win and upon that realisation my senses seemed to open up to the whole experience. I could hear the crowd cheering for my house and I thought about how different it was to the swimming I did on my own. In these cases I would switch off and do length after length in my own world of thought. That was often the appeal – being in the water in my own world – a water-world where body and mind merged into one in the form of another 'sixth' sense. This time, however, I was aware of swimming with the gaze of an entire audience upon me and willing me on to the finish line. Part of me didn't want to finish. I was enjoying the swim and four lengths wasn't enough!

When I got out of the pool and walked back toward the changing room, my English teacher patted me on my shoulder and said, 'Congratulations'. I was aware that she had seen me in a different light and felt pleased that she had said that to me. I heard several others say either 'Well done' or 'Great swim', but I did not feel that attention of this sort was what I really wanted from swimming.

These are distorted reflections, in the way that Sartre (1954) describes. However, they remain vivid for me in that I can still clearly picture the swimming pool and the way that it was transformed during the event by the spectators and the atmosphere that they created. Swimming spaces, whether at sea or in a pool have always remained for me heightened embodied spaces where distinctive sounds (seagulls, waves, amplified sounds rebounding off the water and walls), textures and smells (chlorine, salt water) compete with the visual (still blue water, bright sunshine, fleshy bodies and horizons). So, whereas my adult inter-pretations of these memories are influenced by a more sophisticated reading of the experiences, it is not to suggest that those sensations were not 'lived' at the time. The distortion of the reflection occurs more in the way that I interpret the broader social context of my experiences through contemporary (adult/academic) discourses of childhood, sporting participation, education and embodiment.

The swimming gala was not a major turning point in terms of my 'visibility' in PE lessons, but it was an event that was memorable and meaningful to me in a variety of ways. It made me realise what I really enjoyed about swimming and how I could continue to enjoy it in the way I wanted to. Competitive swimming was not a part of that and I made a subsequent decision that I did not want to join a swimming club. I realised it at that particular moment after the event. I had drawn upon reflections of earlier experiences of swimming, in the sea and at the public pool on a Saturday morning. These experiences were more meaningful to me and were considered in relation to my perception of what training in a swimming club would entail. I had recognised that the embodied enjoyment of being able to engage with swimming on my own terms was more important to me. In subsequent PE lessons, I did not receive any comment about the race from the PE teachers. The football status quo remained, and my end-of-year PE report confirmed that I had remained invisible by noting that I was 'making progress.' All of my friends received these comments and we laughed in the knowledge that the PE teacher who wrote the reports had not been able to distinguish us from one another.

What is interesting, and revealing, as I write about these memories of school sport, is the emotional reaction that it draws from me. Corresponding with Burkitt's (2012) assertion that reflexive practice in research is flooded with the emotional, it has become more apparent to me than I had realised that I am resentful toward the PE teachers at that school. In particular, it was their failure to acknowledge any other ways of being (Hunter 2004) that fuel these emotions. Although I harboured no inclination to be part of an 'elite' group of football players, it was the constant, uncritical reinforcement of a binary based upon *good footballer* and *others* that has remained a source of consternation. In subsequent years, the continued, unchallenged assumption about football as the most 'legitimate' form of sport or PE practice (within the UK) has developed a much greater sense of caution and scepticism whenever I hear claims about the benefits of football, or indeed sport where it is used uncritically as a substitute for football.

It may be the case that many things have changed in the years since I went to school, but my concerns are still fuelled by the knowledge that I was a child who 'loved' sport and thrived in the opportunities provided by my parents and the activities I engaged in outside school. Consequently, my concern is related to the question that if *I* loved sport, what were the experiences like for those children who did not have other opportunities out of school? I was able to compensate for the limited provision in school by my other external activities and was, subsequently, able to build up a reserve of pleasurable memories, ones that would ultimately convince me that school sport was only one small aspect of a much larger 'world of sport'.

My reflections here are shaped by an adult perspective, including those informed by academic sensibilities relating to inclusion and anti-discriminatory practices (Dagkas and Armour 2011, Hayes and Stidder 2012). However, at the time, I did not feel the level of antipathy that infiltrates my thought processes now as I did not have the broader range of experiences to draw upon for comparison. That was the way it was and I managed it the best way that I could. I can see now that I was lucky to have opportunities outside school where I could develop a love of sport and physical activity. However, the reflection about my participation in a school sports 'event' is included as a testament to the importance of additional activities that may provide opportunities to see and experience sport in different ways. My enjoyment of the atmosphere in the swimming pool during the sports day resonates with the excitement described by Tommy in Chapter 3. The way that he enjoyed the sporting activities provided as part of an externally driven, nationally sponsored National School Sport Week, related more to the novelty and thrill of something different. The event may not necessarily have prompted him to take up sport at that very moment, but it might have helped him to, like me, understand what he 'wanted' from sport and enjoyed most about it.

Thinking about childhood memories does not necessarily have to be considered in terms of loss. It is often the case that physical loss of some description is heavily and gainfully used in auto-ethnography to create a greater inward focus of the gaze (Sparkes 1996, Ellis and Bochner 2000) and, ultimately, provides a means to develop a sense of 'otherness' or 'outsiderness'. However, what I have found in my reflections of swimming is that, although continued participation is regulated through externally imposed social control as well as self-enforced control of my body, there are still possibilities to remember those pleasurable moments. Consequently, swimming now provides the opportunity to make those memories more vivid. This is not only through the social act of 'going' swimming, but also in the way that the physical activity, and the sensations that swimming elicits, act as a way of enhancing those memories through an embodied experience. It may be more the case that any sense of 'loss' I feel is more related to the loss of insouciance about the social body and the frustrations felt in relation to the restrictions of adulthood imposed by heightened awareness of bodily hexis (Bourdieu 1990) and the discourses of performativity (Butler 1993) that permeate every aspect of my embodied social being. So, rather than mourning for a loss of innocence it is more likely the case that I rue the loss of times when physical activity did not require a pre-assessment of the physical 'condition' of my body as well as carefully considered strategic planning so as to avert possible social disasters.

Reflections in the gym

The discussion above has focused on childhood memories of sport in and out of school. As an adult, these memories have been influential in the ways that I have prioritised sport as a significant aspect of my leisure time as well as a focus for my academic explorations. 'Doing' sport has remained important and I have attempted to do it throughout my life. Tennis and swimming have remained my main activities, although I have always been willing to attempt other sports if the opportunities arose. More recently, my ageing body has dictated to me the extent to which I can participate. The times of playing tennis everyday are unrealistic, not only because of work and home commitments, but through my body's inability to cope with the physical strains of playing that much. However, a saving grace has always been working out at the gym and it has been during the process of writing this book that I have realised the increasing significance that it has played in my everyday sporting practices.

I had initially started going to the gym in my early twenties when I damaged a tendon in my shoulder while playing tennis. I was advised to strengthen the muscles around my shoulder, as well as adapt the technique of my service action. I was at university in London at that time (in the late 1980s) and started attending a large gym in Covent Garden. The gym was a revelation for me. I had previously considered gyms to be the haunts of bodybuilders, but this one was adopted by a disparate group. They included local workers, dancers, actors, sports enthusiasts and bodybuilders. There was a noticeable gay presence, as it was at a time when bodywork and muscularity were becoming increasingly popular within gay culture (Simpson 1994, Alvarez 2008). However, because of its location, the gym was also frequented by many familiar television personalities and it was exciting to be working out alongside a TV Gladiator or a film star. Consequently, the gym became a space that I enjoyed going to, not only as a means to strengthen my shoulder, but for many other contrasting reasons that related to the negotiation of my social and personal identities. Particularly important for me was the revelation that a 'sporting' space could be one where I could feel more relaxed about bodily and sexual identities. During this time I was playing tennis at a local club. These sports spaces were, however, extremely hegemonic (Connell 2005) and I did not feel that there were opportunities for me to negotiate my sexuality in any other way than by keeping quiet and performing in 'expected' ways (Wellard 2009). That period was spent negotiating a range of separate identities where sport and personal life never really crossed paths. This particular gym offered one space where it felt for me that the two could mix.

It was during that period in the late 1980s that I developed a 'love' of going to the gym. It was in that 'safe' space that I was able to develop the skills (or perform in the manner required) often seen as part of the unwritten rules that determine partic-ipation in other gyms (such as presumption of ability, bodybuilding knowledge and hegemonic displays of sporting masculinity). Consequently, although I have never possessed a bodybuilder's body, my knowledge of the ways to 'perform' within the context of a gym (Fussell 1991, Klein 1993) have meant that I have been able to take part at other gyms during other stages in my life and in various locations in the UK. Working out at the gym has remained the most constant part of my 'sporting' life since that first visit in the 1980s, as there have been many periods when injury has interrupted playing tennis or swimming as much as I would like. Indeed, at the time of writing the final draft of this book, I have been unable to play tennis for several months because of a knee injury. The gym has, once again, provided a much-needed outlet for physical expression in that I am able to adapt my workout routines to the needs of my body and 'work' around my knee as well as incorporate rehabilitation exercises for the specific injury.

Bearing in mind the points above, I thought it would be useful to include a reflection related to the gym. It is often the case that going to the gym is considered in terms of a specific outcome, most often related to 'losing weight' or 'getting fit'. However, my continued participation has never been justified or reasoned in these terms. I go because I enjoy it for a range of reasons in the same way that I play tennis or go swimming for a variety of reasons.

Andrew Sparkes employs auto-ethnographic moments in a gym to explore what he describes as his 'ageing embodiment' (2010: 22). By attempting to make sense of his own experiences at the gym he asserts that he is

> Not only telling stories about my body, but I am telling the stories out of and through my body as a 54 year old, white, heterosexual, middle-class (by dint of profession) male.
>
> (Sparkes 2010: 22)

Sparkes account of his experiences as a regular member of a large corporate gym is revealing in many ways; not only in terms of the personal disclosure that he is able to make about his feelings toward his own body and others at the gym, but also as a social comment about the space of the gym and the technologies of fitness (Pronger 2002) that have increasingly become part of contemporary social-lived (body) practices. However, what is also telling in Sparkes' account is the sense of foreboding relating to the discourses of an ageing body participating in a space increasingly constructed as a domain for a youthful, more 'potent' body. To an extent, although there are similarities in our backgrounds (in that we are both white, middle-class and roughly the same age) there are marked differences in the way that we approach going to the gym. In particular, I have felt that it is the case that I have enjoyed going to the gym *more* as I have become older.

In order to explore the extent of my enjoyment, I thought it would be useful to apply a simple brainstorm exercise about what it is that I actually enjoy about going to the gym. In doing so, I am not merely offering a 'positive spin' on the benefits of going to the gym, but rather I am attempting to unpack the complex subjective permutations and influences that are not always fully taken into consideration. The following is my brainstorm list:

- *I enjoy the actual physical experience of working out.*
- *It is my time and space.*
- *I like 'going' to a designated space – as it makes me do the workout.*
- *It has become part of my routine.*
- *I like to keep fit as it helps me with my other sports.*
- *I want to maintain some form of control over my body as it ages.*
- *I like the feeling of 'being' healthy.*
- *I like the physical sense of building up a sweat and the way my body feels after a workout.*
- *I like being in a place where others are working out and being part of this*

group – but at the same time separate (a different experience from that of other sports I do).

- *I like working out in the winter – as it makes my body feel warm.*
- *I like being aware that I am stronger and fitter than the majority of men my age.*
- *I like being able to watch other people.*
- *I like looking at other bodies.*
- *I like listening to other men talk in the changing rooms – about their wives, girlfriends, children, jobs, sport and bodies (and sometimes about friends who have been sent to prison).*
- *I like showering after I have worked out – when my body is warm. I enjoy the sensation of the shower more so than at home (and in a similar way to liking the shower after playing other sports).*

I am sure I am not the only person who enjoys the physical sensation of working out. I like how my body feels during a workout and there are particular exercises that I enjoy doing more than others. There are times when I am on the treadmill or cross-trainer when a particular song plays on the sound system. It makes me want to dance. Even though I refrain from breaking into dance, I like the exhilarating feeling it gives me and how it makes me step up the intensity of my effort.

Like Sparkes (2010), I enjoy the physical reactions to a workout, such as the sweating and experiencing the differing strains placed upon my body during the exercises. These physical sensations can be understood through a corporeal interpretation in the way that I describe body-reflexive pleasures in Chapter 2. On these occasions, I enjoy feeling that my body is being tested in some way and that I am pushing my body and exploring its limits. However, these specific feelings of enjoyment are based upon a reflexive 'taking stock' of my body at that particular time. There are days when I am feeling healthier than other days. I have learned the signs and draw upon previous experiences to compare them with my current 'condition'. On the occasions when I am feeling healthy, I am like a child and can feel myself walking faster, sometimes feeling the urge to skip or jump and run. The gym provides a space for me to do this without having to feel the 'shame' that Probyn (2005) describes in relation to embodied actions that may be considered as inappropriate in certain social settings.

At other times, when I might feel weaker, there is a correlation between how I feel physically and the way that I perceive my outward social identity. These feelings have occurred throughout my life. It is not something that has happened just in later life. These feelings also draw upon the memories of pleasurable moments that I described in Chapter 2. My memory bank of healthy moments helps me recognise the signs and feelings and, importantly, encourages me to make the most of those moments when I feel healthy. The gym provides a more accessible outlet for responding to the different physiological states of health or 'fitness' that I experience. I am aware that the notion of pushing one's limits both equates with and contradicts Pronger's (2002) descriptions of the contemporary discourses of fitness that I am succumbing to. However, whereas the technologies of fitness that he asserts are creating restricted embodied boundaries, there appears to be also a modicum of agency in that I am aware of those discourses but still feel 'attracted' to the sensations that participating delivers.

Rather than being an oppressive place, the gym provides a specific space, among a variety of spaces, providing a positive experience in my everyday life. It has been interpreted for me in terms of flexibility in comparison with playing tennis or swimming. As I have become older, tennis and swimming have required greater preparation, especially in terms of when, where and how I can play tennis with others or go to a swimming pool, as well as in relation to the physical demands placed upon my body.

Unlike Sparkes (2010), however, I do not see the space of the modern gym as isolating and lonely. Going to the gym, I enjoy that I can be invisible in a way that allows a positive form of self-imposed isolation. Going to the gym is a time and space away from my work and I specifically chose the gym I attend on a regular basis as one that is not part of my university. It is a large gym with many members and I do not know people there by name. I do not want to. In the same way that other people speak about 'escaping' in a large city, I enjoy participating among the other members, but 'on my own'. In particular, for me, the gym provides a different form of enjoyment (one that is ontological, temporal and spatial as well as (anti-) social, physical and psychological) and is a complete contrast to the more social aspects of playing tennis.

As I have aged, I have realised that I enjoy working out at the gym more. A significant factor in this assessment is my awareness that I am less conscious of comparing myself with other men or other bodies in the way I was during my twenties. However, there are still elements of vanity that influence my motivations for participation. I am conscious that I do not want to look like a 'typical' middle-aged man with a large belly. I want to be lithe and flexible in a way that makes me not want to take up too much space or attract attention. There are a number of competing sensibilities here. They relate to my perceptions of power relations, sexuality and heteronormativity. I realise that these are conflicting discourses which operate within the context of heterosexuality and gay masculinity. Sparkes (2010) can be seen to view his participation at the gym within the lens of heteronormativity and possibly with a sense of 'loss' in relation to the construction of the dominant youthful male body and his perception of age removing him from this ideal. The aging body, for him, has created an awareness of his 'outsiderness' through the realisation that his body does not comply with the prevalent discourses of youth operating in the social space of the 'gym'. Although the gay male body has been equally subjected to discourses of the idealised, muscular body (Simpson 1994) and obsession with youth (Edwards 1998),there is a contrast to the heteronormative. Gay cultures and gyms have conflicting messages and not ones that are necessarily replicated within the heteronormative frame that Sparkes describes. Consequently, access to both has allowed me to cope with and negotiate an 'outsider' perspective without the sense of loss that Sparkes describes. I was never an 'insider' in the first place within these heteronormative discourses, although it might be the case that through my embodied practices within the space of the gym, I have *become* more of an insider than I realised.

In addition, I am aware that the sensibilities I have developed as a sociologist have influenced my 'resistance' to presenting (through my bodily hexis) the excesses that I see within the heterosexual matrix (Butler 1993) and in the broader context of western capitalism (Bourdieu 2001, Connell 2007). I have been conscious in my efforts not to project such excesses through either an overdeveloped muscular body or a corpulent (corporate male businessman) body. Staying slim is a way that I feel I am resisting these discourses and helps me convince myself that I am not one of those middle-aged and middle-class fat cats! Consequently, one aspect of my enjoyment of the gym and doing sport, is that I can maintain a particular 'type' of body as well as an inflationary sense of self in the knowledge that I am a lot fitter than many other men my age. However, these egoistic sensibilities are countered by the additional knowledge that even though I am not making efforts to increase muscle mass like a bodybuilder, I am still adopting similar forms of body modification through exercise and diet, and, ultimately, adhering to the forms of body fascism that Pronger (2002) criticises.

Despite being aware of the discourses of self-surveillance that abound within the context of the fitness 'industry', as well as my attempts at trying to understand the reasoning for my continued participation, it remains clear to me that I still enjoy going to gym and taking part in the embodied practice of 'working out'.

7 Conclusions

Sport, fun and enjoyment – the whole package

Nature, so our reasoning mind tells us, could just as easily have given her children all those useful functions of discharging superabundant energy, of relaxing after exertion, of training for the demands of life, of compensating for unfulfilled longings, etc., in the form of purely mechanical exercises and reaction. But no, she gave us play, with its tension, its mirth, and its fun.

(Huizinga 1955: 3)

The ideas in this book have been presented as a stimulus to provoke further discussion on why the topic of fun and enjoyment is important in sport studies (as well as health and body studies) and how these debates fit with existing sport theory. I am not suggesting in any way that what is presented here is a definitive guide to fun and enjoyment in sport, but rather that it may open up the possibility of thinking beyond the margins (Pronger 2002) and assist in working out what we actually want from sport. Like Kirk (2010), who talks about the need to consider the idea of the idea of PE (and ultimately what is wanted from it), and Ahmed (2010), who explores the desire for the desire for happiness, my approach has been to think about thinking about fun and enjoyment in sport and physical activity. The arguments presented in this book suggest that existing theories of the sporting body (and sports participation) in sport studies tend to ignore or fail to consider fully the relevance of embodied pleasure. It is hoped that some of the insights might help how future projects that deal with sporting participation are contemplated and assist thinking about the sporting body and general wellbeing.

This book has not been written in order to provide concrete solutions for how to tackle problems relating to participation in sport and physical activities. Neither has it been about making an attempt to provide universal definitions of fun and enjoyment within the context of sport and physical activity, nor to tell PE teachers and sport practitioners how to go about 'doing' what they do. Rather, the intention has been to open up debate about what fun and enjoyment 'means' to children, young people and adults. In doing so, it is hoped that it will prompt reflection upon how a sporting activity can be experienced as 'fun' in a variety of ways and the importance of recognising fun, enjoyment and pleasure as a central factor in continued participation, particularly at recreational level throughout the life-course.

In this chapter, I focus on several themes that have become apparent during the writing process and are considered to be central to the overall arguments expressed throughout. They are presented here as a way of summarising the key issues relating to thinking about fun and enjoyment in sport and physical activity.

Problems with defining Fun and Enjoyment

I have been attempting to argue in this book that fun and enjoyment are more central to the experience of sport and physical activity than is generally acknowledged. Even though the term fun is complex, it is important to be able to *recognise* that it is complex in the first place. The subjective aspects of fun need to be confronted rather than us uncritically accepting simplistic assumptions that it is either trivial or less serious than other more 'weighty' benefits of engaging in sport. Even when efforts are made to categorise fun and enjoyment within realms of hedonic theorising, that is also misleading, not least because definitions of pleasure and the erotic are more complex than usually credited.

As Kirk (2010) points out in relation to PE, in the UK, the historical construction of PE has produced a specific orientation towards the subject where 'fun' is considered as an aspect which undermines the 'serious' nature of the subject area (and its professional standing, in comparison with other more venerated subjects, such as English and mathematics). The result can be seen (ironically) in the way that PE has opted to operate within a mind/body dualism which has, ultimately affiliated itself with the 'mind' category (rather than embrace an embodied approach). Consequently, fun is considered as a trivial, intrinsically self-motivated, indulgent (and physical) outcome, often associated with children's play or outdated interpretations of egoist drives (in the Freudian sense). Pre-occupation with ideas about how PE should present itself as 'legitimate' has led to a focus upon PE lessons (and sporting activity within school) in terms of assessed outcomes or as a potential career (Wright and Burrows 2006).

For example, by associating fun in sport and physical activity with hedonistic theories and by conflating the object of sporting participation with a career, Bloodworth *et al.* claim that 'to focus on certain forms of pleasant experience, such as fun, may well foreclose other satisfactions associated with exercise, play, games and sport' (2012: 501). However, by attempting to separate fun and enjoyment from other aspects of sport, they fall into the trap of reading 'fun' within a narrow interpretation and, ultimately, present a limited view of what sport should 'look like'. The accounts provided by the children and adults in this book clearly demonstrate that their experiences of sport could not be fully explained as 'just' fun. In doing so, their descriptions of how their experiences were fun for a range of contrasting reasons bear testament to claims that fun and enjoyment are significant aspects for taking part and for future engagement.

Part of the problem with the argument made by Bloodworth *et al.* (2012) is that they claim a focus on fun contributes to an ethical deficit. Apart from their subsequent suggestions for what sport should be like, offering a vision of a rather dry and uninspiring (somewhat puritanical) sporting provision, their arguments contribute to the 'fear of fun' prevalent in schools, as described in Chapter 2.

This is not to suggest, however, that an ethical approach is not valid. Concerns about the possible negative consequences of a purely fun-focused orientation to sport can be alleviated by acknowledgement of the broader dimensions of how fun and enjoyment are experienced. In addition, the significance of responsibility as a factor within an individual's approach to, experience of and continued engagement with sport helps contest claims that fun is merely a shallow pursuit.

In his discussion of freedom and responsibility, Sartre (1954), attempts to counter the problems of existential freedom through the idea that responsibility is a central aspect in the way that an individual makes decisions about how they choose to 'live' in the world. Within the context of fun and enjoyment in sport, fears of hedonistic nihilism are negated by the assumption that an individual has to make decisions about how to engage with, and experience, an activity. Part of this process entails the consideration of potential outcomes or consequences for any actions taken.

> I am responsible for everything, in fact, except for my very responsibility, for I am the foundation of my being. Therefore, everything takes place as if I were compelled to be responsible.
>
> (Sartre 1954: 555)

The idea of fun aligned with responsibility may be a more useful approach than one based in human rights, where it is harder to make obvious connections between demands for individual rights to 'enjoy' sport that are expressed within the same context as issues relating to human suffering and poverty.

What I have been attempting to demonstrate within this book is how fun and enjoyment need to be understood as part of a process of experience, which comprises reflection upon past and present experiences, which then shape decisions about future participation. The broad range of factors influencing how an activity is experienced as fun is assessed in relation to more than individual 'feelings' (either psychological, physical or both) but also individual interpretations of the social (being-for-others), including recognition and assessment of the possible consequences of continued and future participation.

Fun and enjoyment in PE and youth sport contexts

The intention throughout the writing of this book has been to maintain a 'broad' approach (both theoretically and disciplinary). However, it is important to bear in mind the implications and consequences of the way that fun and enjoyment are understood and acted upon within the context of PE and sport provision for young people. As Kirk (2010) suggests, the idea of the idea of PE is up for grabs, but if considered in the light of the potential opportunities or 'freedom' (in the Sartrean sense) it is equally important that well-considered decisions are made about what we want PE and youth sport to look like. Evidence suggests that sport at school remains a defining influence in young people's early experiences of sport, so, PE, and how it is 'delivered', is crucial in an individual's orientation toward sport and future adult participation in it.

It could be claimed that much of what a child learns in Physical Education is generated through an adult PE teacher's formulations of how they think it 'should' be experienced. These formulations are based upon past, positive experiences which are in turn reflected upon favourably (and with pleasure). However, the positive expectations do not have any real resonance if the lived experience of a child does not match up to the ideas promoted by the teacher.

In this case, it is difficult for the circuit of body-reflexive pleasure to be complete without the possibility of the child experiencing the activity positively (and pleasurably) so that informed reflections can be made.

In addition, the orientation to the PE experience is also shaped by the teacher's understanding of their 'role' within the school and all the consequent demands expected in delivering the National Curriculum and current government policy. The focus of much academic research has, with justification, concentrated focus on this particular aspect and the impact of policy upon young lives. However, if taking into consideration the concept of a circuit of interconnected influences, there is a need to recognise how particular orientations toward PE (and the body) are constructed at both the individual and social level.

Bailey *et al.* (2007) in their discussion of wellbeing, suggest that academic debate tends to focus on a distinction between subjective and objective accounts (of pleasure). In particular, an assumption is made that fun, enjoyment and pleasure, because of their subjective nature, are best explained through hedonistic theories which, in turn, ultimately equate wellbeing with a certain quality of experience and because of this are demeaned by this association. However, it is problematic to make such clear divisions and, particularly in education, it appears the focus on childhood wellbeing, as mentioned above, has reinforced dualistic thinking about the body, which is then interpreted in terms of a 'creative' mind in opposition to a potentially sinful body (which needs to be controlled). As the examples described in this book have shown, there is an important social and 'learning' element involved in sporting activities. This can be seen as a particular form of learning and at the same time a learning about one's own body, as well as about understanding and placing that experience within a social context.

If taking into account the process of body-reflexive pleasures, it becomes clearer that a narrow form of intrinsic, subjective pleasure is only part of the picture as other factors take equal, if not greater precedence. This is particularly the case with initial experiences of sporting activity, especially within the context of school sports and physical education. Here, pleasure in its subjective form *is* essential to the development of a positive orientation to both the individual body and sporting participation.

Lawrence (2006) suggests that experiences formed during school ultimately impact on young people's decisions to continue with physical activity. Similarly, many physical educationalists believe that enjoyable physical education experiences are necessary in developing positive attitudes towards PE (Prochaska *et al.* 2003, Subramanian and Silverman 2002). However, Dismore (2007), in her study of school children's attitudes to PE, found that the general enjoyment of PE did not automatically stop in the first year of secondary school. Rather, the practices and focus of provision for PE and school sports shifted the emphasis to more adult-centred, competitive sports, taught by more-skilled, specialised PE staff. The focus became more 'ability' and performance based and ultimately made the children reflect upon their bodies in terms of whether they felt 'able' to take part or not (Wellard 2006b). Consequently, there is a movement toward a more narrow view of fun, developed in primary school settings, where educational practitioners in secondary settings align with more traditional readings of fun, which is invariably seen as an inappropriate outcome of PE (Siedentop *et al.* 1986). However, it could be claimed that restricting the fun element and the potential for pleasurable experiences (which can be, in turn, reflected upon positively) not only diminishes the possibility of broader engagement with the body, but also restricts opportunities to develop more creative approaches to the learning process.

Wright (2004) provides a further reasoned argument for a broader understanding of fun and pleasure by exploring the importance of recognising the value of happiness in primary school PE. Drawing upon the philosophical interpretations of pleasure and happiness by Aristotle, Kant and Mill where truth, goodwill and general happiness are core values, Wright suggests that these ideas remain relevant today. Whereas much of contemporary PE is focused on developing skills, Wright asserts that mastery as well as enjoyment are both necessary and complimentary.

It is apparent that young people need to have a range of experiences of sport in order to be able to make distinctions about what was considered pleasurable for them. However, it is not just about providing the opportunity to 'have a go' in order to comply with curriculum directives. It is about providing opportunities for young people to experience activities and make assessments about when, where and how an activity is pleasurable. Importantly, there need to be personal assessments of how this pleasure was experienced, whether it was gained through mastery, as Wright (2004) describes, as a physical thrill or as a sense of psychological achievement. Whatever way, the body-reflexive process constructs an orientation toward, in this case, sporting activity and, ultimately, the creation of positive reflections which can be drawn upon at any time.

If taking into consideration the importance of recognising the circuit of body-reflexive pleasures, it could be claimed that the teacher and the school-based environment contribute significantly to the collection of pleasurable experiences. The teacher is particularly important in this process, as they need to be able to remember, themselves, the multiple ways in which a sporting activity can be experienced as fun. Part of this process is to reflect upon personal experiences of sport so that they do not risk complacency by forgetting that the activities they teach need to be experienced positively in the first place.

Ultimately, for children and adults, pleasure needs to be recognised, unpacked and reflected upon so that a reflexive approach to the body can be applied. Children (as well as adults) need to 'learn' what to look for and how to enjoy their bodies. As Mark Vernon suggests,

> In general, there is a need to assess different pleasures for happiness-as-positive-emotion to work, and establish which are likely to lead to the greatest happiness, and therefore which are the best to cultivate.
>
> Vernon (2008: 19)

In order to do this, we need to escape from simplistic readings of fun and enjoyment and recognise the range of pleasures available in sport and physical activity in order to be able to promote positive (pleasurable) experiences for young people. In doing so, we allow them to reflect upon their experiences and make reasoned decisions about further participation. Awareness of the circuit of body-reflexive pleasures is suggested as a possible starting point.

Recognising the whole package of sport

For children and young people, participation in sport is often expressed in terms of the potential for fun, rather than as an emotional reaction that occurs during the activity. The notion that activity is considered in terms of 'it *will* be' or 'it *was*' fun suggests that a broader 'process' is in operation rather than a one-off moment of subjective gratification. The simplistic perception that fun is trivial undermines the diverse ways that children anticipate, then experience and reflect upon, the fun elements within a sporting activity. Anticipation of fun may relate to many things, such as potential achievement, learning something new, an embodied experience or a thrill. In whatever way, they add to a personal memory bank, as experiences in themselves and as an additional contribution to identity assessment. Understood in this way, even a hedonistic experience can be seen as significant if considered in relation to its contribution to the memory bank of pleasurable moments and its impact on how the individual makes assessments about future participation.

However, in recognising the broader dimensions of fun and enjoyment, it is also necessary to acknowledge the broader dimensions of sport and physical activity experience, or the whole package of sport. I have attempted to demonstrate that participation in a sporting activity is influenced by a range of competing and conflicting factors. Successful participation often relies upon awareness of the 'full contents' of the package and then navigation of the social, cultural, psychological and physiological expectations demanded for access to participation and continued participation. All of these contribute to the varying ways that an individual is allowed entry (to a particular sporting activity) and, once in, is able to enjoy the experience.

Take, for instance, the example that I have been incorporating within this book of tennis. To get to the stage of experiencing the pleasurable aspects of actually playing the game, there is a process of learning, understanding and interpreting what tennis signifies within one's immediate social, political and geographical situation. This process involves an understanding of the relationship of one's embodied self to a socially constructed form of physical, adult play (sport). Consideration of one's physical body, gender, age and race have to be applied to general perceptions of who is considered 'able' to play. This is not to say that participation is excluded from the start in certain cases, but awareness of the 'entry stakes' ultimately orientates the individual to make assumptions about whether they will be welcome or not.

My introduction to tennis was through my parents and during these early experiences I was able to 'learn' more than just the technical skills of how to play; also the social rules and etiquette expected within the game. Consequently, later attempts to join tennis clubs (in order to play a sport that I enjoyed) were uneventful in that I was able to demonstrate my knowledge of the whole package and 'fit in'. My point is that 'becoming' a fully fledged member of a sports club requires conformity of some sort, which means adapting to further 'rules' and codes of play, much like a 'hidden curriculum' (Fernandez-Balboa 1993) of sport that operates in addition to taken-for-granted prerequisites such as an ability to play the game. Seen in this light, it is not only the young person that is restricted by operating within adult discourses of what school-based sport should look like. So too is the adult in the way that they have only certain outlets in which to be able to express these embodied feelings because of the way that many forms of club sport are internally 'policed' (in terms of, for instance, age, ability, gender, class and race).

The hidden curriculum of many sports may also be a reason for the popularity among many adults for more individual pursuits, such as running, cycling and swimming. For both Gary and Elizabeth, introduced in Chapter 5, swimming and running (respectively) were activities they initially took up because they could do them on their own. Although, in both cases, over a period of time, increased confidence in their ability as well as a process of 'learning' to become a 'swimmer' and a 'runner' meant that the social elements increased. In Elizabeth's case, she joined a running club so that she could take part in races.

At the same time, the social codes of etiquette are not the only contents within the whole package. Much of the appeal of many club-based sports is the additional pre- and post-match social activities. Rituals, hazing, initiation rites and drinking games can all add to, if not play a central part in, a sense of belonging to a group (Johnson 2011) and, possibly, what an individual enjoys most in taking part. In many cases, the social activities contribute more continued participation than actually playing the sport. Jodie, presented in Chapter 4, was quite open in her assessment that taking part in the boccia club was, for her, about the social aspects and the opportunity to meet and make friends, to the extent that she admitted that it did not matter what the sporting activity was, rather the broader 'package' was more important.

If we recognise that there are other (covert and open) factors operating in any sporting activity, the suggestion is, therefore, that there is the case to be made for children and young people to be made more aware of them. For it may be that teaching only the skills required to 'play' is not enough to guarantee further and future participation.

To sum up, it is clear that fun and enjoyment are central factors in whether a sporting activity is experienced positively. However, it is also suggested that individual assessments about the 'whole package' of a particular sport contribute to whether an individual considers it possible to be able to experience participation as enjoyable and, subsequently, whether participation or continued participation is either possible or worthwhile.

Although the contexts in which children, young people and adults are able to access sport are different, particularly in terms of the prescriptive nature of school-based sport in comparison with the relatively greater opportunities available to adults, the ways in which assessments are made about participation are invariably similar in that fun and enjoyment are major influences. Part of the process in making assessments about future participation is by drawing upon previous positive (enjoyable) experiences in order to make conscious decisions about whether to continue or not.

Consequently, central to the arguments put forward in this book is that reflection upon when, how and why an experience in a sporting activity was fun needs to be made in order to be able to develop a positive orientation toward the activity. The reflection is part of the process in a circuit of body-reflexive pleasure where anticipation, experience and reflection – influenced by a range of social, psychological and physiological factors – contribute to continued participation. The significance of an embodied approach to fun and enjoyment in sporting activities cannot be ignored.

Last week, and only a few days before I was due to submit the final draft of this book to the publishers, I had a break from writing and went down to my tennis club. The sun had popped out and, after what seemed like an endless, cold and grey winter I felt that I should get outside for an hour or so. I thought it would be an opportunity to take on the ball machine and test out my knee, as I hadn't picked up a tennis racquet for three months after injuring it during a friendly doubles match.

I don't know whether the process of writing about pleasurable moments has influenced my frame of mind, but while driving down to the club I couldn't contain my excitement that I was about to play tennis again. Three months not playing seemed such a long time. Although I had slight worries about whether playing now would aggravate the injury, I thought that by using the ball machine I wouldn't have to run around too much. During the drive down to the courts, my mind was not on negative thoughts, but rather it was awash with previous pleasurable memories of playing and how I might be able to recapture some of those. It was a thrill to get that 'buzz' of anticipation again and the possibility that, maybe, I could hit another 'backhand down the line' and add it to my memory bank of pleasurable sporting moments.

References

Agassi, A. (2009) *Open: An Autobiography*. London: Harper Collins.

Ahmed, S. (2010) *The Promise of Happiness*. Durham, NC: Duke University Press.

Aitchison, C. (2003) 'From leisure and disability to disability leisure: Developing data, definitions and discourses', *Disability & Society*, 18 (7), 955–69.

Alcock, P. (2006) *Understanding Poverty*. Basingstoke: Palgrave Macmillan.

Allen-Collinson, J. (2009) 'Sporting embodiment: Sports studies and the (continuing) promise of phenomenology', *Qualitative Research in Sport and Exercise*, 1 (3), 270–6.

Alvarez, E. (2008) *Muscle Boys: Gay Gym Culture*. New York: Routledge.

Bailey, R. and Morley, D. (2003) 'Talented pupils in physical education – An inclusive approach', *Gifted and Talented Update*, Issue 5.

Arbour, K., Latimer, A., Martin, K. and Jung, M. (2007) 'Moving beyond the stigma: The impression formation benefits of exercise for individuals with a physical disability', *Adapted Physical Education Quarterly*, 24 (2), 144–59.

Atkinson, M. (2010) 'Fell running in post-sport territories', *Qualitative Research in Sport and Exercise*, 2 (2), 109–32.

Bailey R. (2005) 'Physical education, sport and social inclusion', *Educational Review*, 57 (1), 71–90.

Bailey R., Armour, K., Kirk, D., Jess, M., Pickup, I. and Sandford, R. (2009) 'The educational benefits claimed for physical education and school sport: An academic review', *Research Papers in Education*, 24 (1), 1–27.

Bailey, R., McNamee, M. and Bloodworth, A. (2007) 'Sport, well-being and gender' in I. Wellard (ed.), *Rethinking Gender and Youth Sport*. London: Routledge.

Ball, S. (2004) 'Performativities and fabrications in the education economy: Towards the performative society' in S. Ball (ed.), *The RoutledgeFalmer Reader in Sociology of Education*. London: RoutledgeFalmer.

Barton, L. (2004) 'The disability movement: Some observations' in J. Swain *et al.* (eds), *Disabling Barriers – Enabling Environments*. London: Sage.

Berthelot, G., Len, S., Hellard, P., Tafflet, M., Guillaume, M., Vollmer, J.-C., Gager, B., Quinquis, L., Marc, A. and Toussaint, J.-F. (2011) 'Exponential growth combined with exponential decline explains lifetime performance evolution in individual and human species', *AGE*, 2011 (DOI: 10.1007/s11357-011-9274-9).

Bloodworth, A., McNamee, M. and Bailey, R. (2012) 'Sport, physical activity and well-being: an objectivist account', *Sport, Education and Society*, 17 (4), 497–514.

Booth, D. (2009) 'Politics and pleasure: The philosophy of physical education revisited', *Quest*, 61, 133–53.

Bourdieu, P. (1986) *Distinction*. London: Routledge.

——(1990) *The Logic of Practice*. Cambridge: Polity Press.

——(2001) *Masculine Domination*. Cambridge: Polity Press.

Bourdieu, P. and Wacquant, L. (1992) *An Invitation to Reflexive Sociology*. Cambridge: Polity Press.

Brown, T. and Payne, G. (2009) 'Conceptualizing the phenomenology of movement in physical education: Implications for pedagogical inquiry and development', *Quest*, 61, 418–41.

Burkitt, I. (2012) 'Emotional reflexivity: Feeling, emotion and imagination in reflexive dialogues', *Sociology*, 46 (3), 458–72.

Butler, J. (1993) *Bodies that Matter*. New York: Routledge.

Butler, S., Gross, J. and Hayne, P. (1995) 'The effect of drawing on memory performance in young children', *Developmental Psychology*, 31 (4), 597–608.

Chatzisarantis, N., Hagger, M., Biddle, S. and Karageorghis, C. (2002) 'The cognitive processes by which perceived locus of causality predicts participation in physical activity', *Journal of Health Psychology*, 7, 685–99.

Christensen, P. and James, A. (2008) 'Childhood diversity and commonality: Some methodological insights' in P. Christensen and A. James (eds), *Research with Children: Perspectives and Practices*. London: RoutledgeFalmer.

Connell, R. (2005) *Masculinities*. Cambridge: Polity Press.

——(2007) *Southern Theory*. Cambridge: Polity Press.

Crabbe, T., Bailey, G., Blackshaw, T., Brown, A., Choak, C., Gidley, B., Mellor, G., O'Connor, K., Slater, I. and Woodhouse, D. (2006) *Knowing the Score: Positive Futures Case Study Research: Final Report*. London: Home Office.

Csikszentmihalyi, M. (1990) *Flow: The Psychology of Optimal Experience*. New York: Harper and Row.

Dagkas, S. and Armour, K. (2011) *Inclusion and Exclusion Through Youth Sport*. London: Routledge.

Deci, E. and Ryan, R. (2000) 'The "What" and "Why" of goal pursuits: Human needs and the self-determination of behavior', *Psychological Inquiry*, 11, 227–68.

DePalma, R. and Atkinson, E. (2006) 'The sound of silence: Talking about sexual orientation and schooling', *Sex Education*, 6 (4), 333–49.

DePauw, K. (1997) 'The (In)Visability of DisAbility: Cultural contexts and "sporting bodies"', *Quest*, 49 (4), 416–30.

Dimen, M. (2003) *Sexuality, Intimacy, Power*. New York: Routledge.

Dionigi, R., Horton, S. and Baker, J. (2011) 'Negotiations of the ageing process: Older adults' stories of sports participation', *Sport, Education and Society*, 2011, 1–18 (iFirst article).

Dismore. H. (2007) 'The Attitudes of Children and Young People Towards Physical Education and School Sport, With Particular Reference to the Transition from Key Stage 2 to Key Stage 3', unpublished PhD thesis, Canterbury Christ Church University.

Dismore, H. and Bailey, R. (2011) 'Fun and enjoyment in physical education: Young people's attitudes', *Research Papers in Education*, 26 (4), 499–516.

Dornan, P., Flaherty, J. and Veit-Wilson, J. (2004) *Poverty: The Facts.* London: Child Poverty Action Group.

Dudley, D., Okely, A., Pearson, P., Cotton, W. and Penney, D. (2011) 'A systematic review of the effectiveness of physical education and school sport interventions targeting physical activity, movement skills and enjoyment of physical activity', *European Physical Education Review*, 17 (3), 353–78.

Edwards, T. (1998) 'Queer fears: Against the cultural turn', *Sexualities*, 1 (4), 471–84.

Ellis, C. and Bochner, A. (2000) 'Autoethnography, personal narrative, reflexivity' in N. Denzin and Y. Lincoln (eds), *Handbook of Qualitative Research* (Second Edition). Thousand Oaks: Sage.

Ereaut, G. and Whiting, R. (2008) *What do we mean by 'wellbeing'? And why might it matter?* DCSF Research Report, DCSF-RW073.

Evans, J., Davies, B. and Wright, J. (2004) *Body Knowledge and Control.* London: Routledge.

Evans, J., Rich, E., Allwood, R. and Davies, B. (2007) 'Being 'able' in a performative culture: Physical education's contribution to a healthy interest in sport' in I. Wellard (ed.), *Rethinking Gender and Youth Sport*. London: Routledge.

Featherstone, M., and Hepworth, M. (1991) 'The mask of ageing and the postmodern life course' in M. Featherstone, M. Hepworth, and B. Turner (eds), *The Body: Social Process and Cultural Theory*. London: Sage.

M. Featherstone, M. Hepworth, and B. Turner (eds), *The Body: Social Process and Cultural Theory*. London: Sage.

Fernandez-Balboa, J-M. (1993) 'Socio-cultural characteristics of the hidden curriculum in physical education, *Quest*, 45, 230–54.

Firestone, S. (1979) *The Dialectic of Sex: The Case for Feminist Revolution.* London: The Women's Press.

Foucault, M. (1976) *The History of Sexuality, Volume 1*. New York: Vintage.

Fussell, S. (1991) *Muscle*. London: Abacus.

Gard, M. and Wright, J. (2005) *The Obesity Epidemic: Science, Morality and Ideology*. London: Routledge.

Gibbons, K. (2006) *New Opportunities in PE and Sport: A case study evaluation of the impact of NOPES funding on disaffected youth*. London: Big Lottery Fund.

Goffman, E. (1972) *Encounters*. Harmondsworth: Penguin.

Gold, J. and Gold, M. (2007) 'Access for all: The rise of the Paralympic Games', *The Journal of the Royal Society for the Promotion of Health*, 2007, 127 (3), 137–41.

Graham, G. (1995) 'Physical education through students' eyes and in students' voices: Implications for teachers and researchers', *Journal of Teaching in Physical Education*, 14 (4), 478–82.

Green, K., Smith, A., Thurston, M. and Lamb, K. (2007) 'Gender and secondary school National Curriculum physical education: Change alongside continuity' in I. Wellard (ed.), *Rethinking Gender and Youth Sport*. London: Routledge.

Guttmann, A. (1996) *The Erotic in Sport*. New York: Columbia University Press.

Hagger, M. and Chatzisarantis, N. (2005) 'First- and higher-order models of attitudes, normative influence, and perceived behavioural control in the Theory of Planned Behaviour', *British Journal of Social Psychology*, 44, 513–35.

Hagger, M. and Chatzisarantis, N. (2009) 'Integrating the theory of planned behaviour and self-determination theory in health behaviour: A meta-analysis', *British Journal of Health Psychology*, 14, 275–302.

Hargreaves, J. (1986) *Sport, Power and Culture*. London: Polity Press.

Hayes, G. and Stidder, G. (2012) *Equity and Inclusion in Physical Education and Sport* (Second Edition). Abingdon: Routledge.

Heikkala, J. (1993) 'Discipline and excel: Techniques of the self and body and the logic of competing', *Sociology of Sport Journal*, 10, 397–412.

Hoult, E. (2009) 'Resilience in Adult Learners', unpublished PhD, University of Kent.

Huizinga, J. (1955) *homo ludens.* Boston: Beacon Press.

ـــ. (2010) *Third Age and Leisure Research: Principles and Practice.* ـــne: Leisure Studies Publications.

ـــr, L. (2004) 'Bourdieu and the social space of the PE class: Reproduction of doxa through practice', *Sport, Education and Society*, 9 (2), 175–92.

Jeanes, R. (2010) '"It lets us be a 'normal' family": The value of inclusive play facilities for addressing social exclusion amongst young disabled people and their families' in M. Stuart-Hoyle and J. Lovell (eds), *Leisure Experiences: Space, Place and Performance.* Eastbourne: Leisure Studies Publications.

Jenks, C. (2005) *Childhood.* Abingdon: Routledge.

Johnson, J. (2011) 'Across the threshold: A comparative analysis of communitas and rites of passage in sport hazing and initiations', *Canadian Journal of Sociology*, 36 (3), 199–226.

Kehler, M. and Atkinson, M. (2010) *Boys' Bodies: Speaking the Unspoken.* New York: Peter Lang Publishing.

Kirk, D. (2006) 'The "obesity crisis" and school physical education', *Sport, Education and Society*, 11 (2), 121–34.

ـــ(2010) *Physical Education Futures.* Abingdon: Routledge.

Klein, A. (1993) *Little Big Men: Bodybuilding subculture and gender construction.* Albany: State University of New York Press.

Knowles, Z. and Gilbourne, D. (2010) 'Aspiration, inspiration and illustration: Initiating debate on reflective practice writing', *The Sport Psychologist*, 24, 504–20.

Kumari Campbell, F. (2008) 'Exploring internalized ableism using critical race theory', *Disability & Society*, 23 (2), 151–62.

Kvale, S. (1996) *InterViews.* Thousand Oaks: Sage.

Landry, F. (1995) 'Paralympic Games and social integration' in M. de Moragas and M. Botella (eds), *The Keys of Success: The social, sporting, economic and communications impact of Barcelona '92.* Bellaterra: Servei de Publicacions de la UAB.

Laureus (2009) *Breaking the Cycle of Violence.* London: Laureus.

Lawrence, J. (2006) 'Negotiating Change: The impact of school transfer on attainment, self-esteem, self-motivation and attitudes in physical education', unpublished doctoral dissertation, Brunel University.

Lefebvre, H. (1991) *The Production of Space.* Oxford: Blackwell.

Light, R. and Wallian, N. (2008) 'A constructivist-informed approach to teaching swimming', *Quest*, 60 (3), 387–404.

London East Research Institute (2007). *A Lasting Legacy for London? Assessing the legacy of the Olympic Games and Paralympic Games.* London: Greater London Authority.

MacPhail, A., Kinchin, G. and Kirk, D. (2003) 'Students' conceptions of sport and sport education', *European Physical Education Review*, 9 (3), 285–99.

Maivorsdotter, N. and Lundvall, S. (2009) 'Aesthetic experience as an aspect of embodied learning: Stories from physical education student teachers', *Sport, Education and Society*, 14 (3), 265–79.

Massey, D. (2005) *for space.* London: Sage.

McKay, J., Messner, M. and Sabo, D. (2000) *Masculinities, Gender Relations and Sport.* London: Sage.

McNamee, M. (2005) 'The nature and values of physical education' in K. Green and K. Hardman, *Physical Education: Essential Issues.* London: Sage.

Miller, T. (1995) 'A Short History of the Penis', *Social Text*, 43, 1–26.

ـــ(2001) *Sportsex.* Philadelphia: Temple University Press.

Nettleton, S. and Hardey, M. (2006) 'Running away with health: The urban marathon and the construction of "charitable bodies"', *Health: An Interdisciplinary Journal for the Social Study of Health, Illness and Medicine*, Vol. 10 (4), 441–60 (DOI: 10.1177/1363459306067313 1363-4593).

Nichols, G. (2007) *Sport and Crime Reduction: The role of sports in tackling youth crime*. London: Routledge.

Owen, G. (2006) 'Emotions and Identities in Sport: Gay Pride and Shame in Competitive Rowing', unpublished PhD, London South Bank University.

Petchesky, R. (1986) *Abortion and Woman's Choice: The State, Sexuality and Reproductive Freedom*. London: Verso.

Phoenix, C. and Orr, N. (2012) 'Moving Stories: Physical Activity and Ageing', presentation at BSA, Ageing, Body and Society Study Group Conference, British Library Conference Centre, London, 6 July 2012.

Pickard, A. (2007) 'Girls, bodies and pain: Negotiating the body in ballet', in I. Wellard (ed.), *Rethinking Gender and Youth Sport*. London: Routledge.

Plummer, K. (1983) *Documents of Life*. London: Allen & Unwin.

——(2010) *Sociology: The Basics*. Abingdon: Routledge.

Powell, S. and Wellard, I. (2008) *Policies and Play: The impact of national policies on children's opportunities for play*. London: Play England and the National Children's Bureau.

Pringle, A., Zwolinsky, S., Smith, A., Robertson, S., McKenna, J. and White, A. (2011) 'The pre-adoption demographic and health profiles of men participating in a programme of men's health delivered in English Premier League football clubs', *Public Health*, 125, 411–16.

Pringle, R. (2009) 'Defamiliarizing heavy-contact sports: A critical examination of rugby, discipline and pleasure', *Sociology of Sport Journal*, 26, 211–34.

Probyn, E. (2005) *Blush: Faces of shame*. Sydney: University of New South Wales Press.

Prochaska, J. and DiClemente, C. (2005) 'The transtheoretical approach' in J. Norcross and M. Goldfried (eds), *Handbook of Psychotherapy Integration* (Second Edition). New York: Oxford University Press.

Prochaska, J., Sallis, J., Slymen, D. and McKenzie, T. (2003) 'A longitudinal study of children's enjoyment of physical education', *Pediatric Exercise Science*, 15, 170–8.

Pronger, B. (1990) *The Arena of Masculinity*. London: GMP Publishers.

——(2002) *Body Fascism: Salvation in the Technology of Fitness*. Toronto: University of Toronto Press.

Rowe, D. (1999) *Sport, Culture and the Media*. Buckingham: Open University Press.

Runswick-Cole K. and Goodley D. (2011) 'Problematising policy: conceptions of "child", "disabled" and "parents" in social policy in England', *International Journal of Inclusive Education*, 15 (1).

Sallis, J. and Owen, N. (1999) *Physical Activity and Behavioral Medicine*. Thousand Oaks. Sage.

Sandford, R., Armour, K. and Duncombe, R. (2008) 'Physical activity and personal/social development for disaffected youth in the UK: In search of evidence' in N. Holt (ed.), *Positive Youth Development Through Sport*. Abingdon: Routledge.

Sartre, J-P. (1954) *Being and Nothingness*. New York: Philosophical Library.

Shakespeare, T. (2006). *Disability Rights and Wrongs*. London: Routledge.

Shilling, C. (1993) *The Body and Social Theory*. London: Sage.

Siedentop, D., M and, C. and Taggart, A. (1986) *Physical Education: Teaching and curriculum strategies for grades 5–12*. Palo Alto: Mayfield.

Silverman, D. (1989) 'Telling convincing stories: A plea for cautious positivism in case-studies' in B. Glassner and J. Moreno (eds), *The Qualitative-Quantitative Distinction in the Social Sciences*. Norwell: Kluwer Academic Publishers.

Simpson, M. (1994) *Male Impersonators*. London: Cassell.

Smith, J. (2007) 'The first rush of movement: A phenomenological preface to movement education', *Phenomenology and Practice* 1 (1), 47–75.

Soja, E. (1999) *Thirdspace: Journeys to Los Angeles and other real-and-imagined places.* Oxford: Blackwell.

Sparkes, A. (1996) 'The fatal flaw: A narrative of the fragile body-self', *Qualitative Inquiry*, 2, 463–94.

——(2002) *Telling Tales in Sport and Physical Activity: A Qualitative Journey*. Champaign: Human Kinetics Press.

——(2010) 'Performing the ageing body and the importance of place: Some autoethnographic moments' in B. Humberstone (ed.), *Third Age and Leisure Research: Principles and Practice.* Eastbourne: Leisure Studies Publications.

Stanley, L. (1993) 'On Auto/Biography in Sociology', *Sociology*, 27 (1), 41–52.

Stebbins, R. (2006) *Serious Leisure: A Perspective of Our Time.* New Jersey: Transaction Publishers.

Storey, D. (1960) *This Sporting Life*. London: Vintage.

Stott, M. (2011) *The Big Society Challenge*. Thetford: Keystone Development Trusts Publications.

Subramanian, P. and Silverman, S. (2002) 'Using complimentary data: An investigation of student attitude in physical education', *Journal of Sport Pedagogy*, 8, 74–91.

Svoboda, B. (1994) *Sport and physical activity as a socialisation environment: Scientific review Part 1.* Strasbourg: Council of Europe.

Synnott, A. (1993) *The Body Social*. London: Routledge.

Tinning, R. (2010) *Pedagogy and Human Movement: Theory, practice, research.* London: Routledge.

Tomlinson, A. (1990) *Consumption, Identity and Style*. London: Routledge.

Trost, S., Owen, N., Bauman, A., Sallis, J. and Brown, W. (2002) 'Correlates of adults' participation in physical activity: Review and update', *Medicine & Science in Sports & Exercise*, 34 (12), 1996–2001.

Twigg, J. (2004) 'The body, gender, and age: Feminist insights', *Journal of Aging Studies*, 18, 59–73.

UNICEF (2007) *Child poverty in perspective: An overview of child well-being in rich countries.* Innocenti Report Card 7. Florence: UNICEF Innocenti Research Centre.

Urry, J. (1995) *Consuming Places.* London: Routledge

Vernon, M. (2008) *Wellbeing*. Stocksfield: Acumen.

Weed, M. (2006) 'The story of an ethnography: The experience of watching the 2002 World Cup in the pub', *Soccer and Society,* 7 (1), 76–95.

Weed, M., Coren, E., Fiore, J. with Mansfield, L., Wellard, I., Chatziefstathiou, D. and Dowse, S. (2009) *A Systematic Review of the Evidence Base for Developing a Physical Activity and Health Legacy from the London 2012 Olympic and Paralympic Games.* London: Department of Health.

Weed, M., Mansfield, L. and Dowse, S. (2010) *Active Celebration: Using the London 2012 Games to get the Nation Moving.* London: Department of Health.

Wellard, I. (2002) 'Men, sport, body performance and the maintenance of "exclusive masculinity"', *Leisure Studies*, 21, 235–47.

——(2006a) 'Exploring the limits of queer and sport' in J. Caudwell (ed.) *Sport, Sexualities and Queer Theory: Challenges and controversies*. London: Routledge.

——(2006b) 'Able bodies and sport participation: Social constructions of physical ability', *Sport, Education and Society*, 11 (2).

——(2007) *Rethinking Gender and Youth Sport*. London: Routledge.

——(2009) *Sport, Masculinities and the Body*. New York: Routledge.

——(2012) 'Body-reflexive pleasures: Exploring bodily experiences within the context of sport and physical activity', *Sport, Education and Society*, 17 (1).

Whaley, D. and Schrider, A. (2005) 'The process of adult exercise adherence: Self-perceptions and competence', *The Sport Psychologist*, 19, 148–63.

Wheaton, B. (2004) *Understanding Lifestyle Sports: Consumption, identity and difference*. London: Routledge.

Whitehead, M. (2010) *Physical Literacy: Throughout the lifecourse*. London: Routledge.

Winance, M. (2007) 'Being normally different? Changes to normalization processes: From alignment to work on the norm', *Disability & Society*, 22 (6), 625–38.

Woodward, K. (1991). *Aging and its discontents: Freud and other fictions*. Bloomington: Indiana University Press.

Wright, J. and Burrows, L. (2006) 'Re-conceiving ability in physical education', *Sport, Education and Society*, 11 (2), 275–92.

Wright, L. (2004) 'Preserving the value of happiness in physical education', *Physical Education and Sport Pedagogy*, 9 (2), 149–63.

Zarrett, N., Lerner, R., Carrano, J., Fay, K., Peltz, J. and Li, Y. (2008) 'Variations in adolescent engagement in sports and its influence on positive youth development' in N. Holt (ed.), *Positive Youth Development Through Sport*. Abingdon: Routledge.

Index